War and Weapons

Sampson Low

Contents

Left top: A battalion of Swedish troops stationed with the UN forces in the Sinai Desert.
Left centre: A Japanese samurai warrior in his elaborate yet functional armour.
Left bottom: Detail from a painting of Napoleon's retreat from Moscow, 1812.
Cover: A Chieftain tank, and in the foreground a flintlock musket of the 18th century.

Editorial

Editorial adviser
Mike Blanch
Keeper of Education,
National Army Museum,
London

Editor
Jennifer L. Justice

Illustrations
Angus McBride
Dick Eastland
Michael Trim

NATIONAL ARMY MUSEUM
The original text was prepared by the staff of the National Army Museum, London, and we wish to thank the museum's Director for this assistance.

Designed and Produced by Grisewood & Dempsey Ltd.
Paulton House, 8 Shepherdess Walk, London N.1

Published by Sampson Low,
Berkshire House, Queen Street, Maidenhead

SBN 562 00040 2

© Grisewood & Dempsey Ltd., 1976

Made and printed in Great Britain by Purnell and Sons Limited
Paulton (Avon) and London

War and Weapons

Warfare is an inseparable part of human history. Whether fought for greed, conquest, or an ideology, wars have taken their toll in destruction and human suffering. But as a part of our history the study of warfare can tell us a great deal about the development of society. Many important scientific and technological advances have been direct results of military rivalry.

War and Weapons traces the history of warfare from the first organized armies in Mesopotamia to the military might of modern nuclear weapons. Though there have been some similarities between the armed conflicts in every century, the nature of war has changed significantly since the days of slings and arrows. Armies were revolutionized by the introduction of gunpowder in the Middle Ages; as warfare became more complex, strategy and tactics emerged as a serious study. In the last 60 years aerial warfare has developed dramatically; modern warfare is a co-ordinated effort between the forces of land, sea, and air. A fighting unit is only as good as the individuals within it; the welfare of the private soldier has only received serious consideration in relatively modern times. Today's standing armies are highly technical, mechanized forces backed by a terrifying arsenal of nuclear weapons.

Above: The all-enclosing bascinet which protected the head and face.
Below: Two modern jet fighter-bombers with their armaments.

Man the Aggressor

Despite the incredibly technical nature of modern combat, many of warfare's basic characteristics have changed little since ancient times.

Whether for greed or conquest, survival or an ideology, Man has always been aggressive. The study of the recorded history of warfare from minor skirmishes to full-scale battles tells us a great deal about the constructive and destructive sides of human nature. It also reveals much about the developments of society and the advances in technology which are often spurred on by military rivalry.

Classical warfare
In primitive societies fighting was often a simple matter of surprise attack followed by quick retreat. Today, warfare is complex, sophisticated, and highly technical. But certain similarities can still be found between armed struggles literally hundreds of years apart.

The first organized armies appeared in ancient Mesopotamia, where battles, fought by the mutual agreement of the opposing commanders, were a matter of individual combat once the armies had been led on to the field. Mobility was added in the form of chariots and later cavalry. Commanders soon found that they gained the advantage if they could force a confrontation when the enemy was unprepared or at a tactical disadvantage.

Classical warfare changed little until gunpowder was introduced into Europe and the first firearms appeared in the 14th century. These new weapons revolutionized warfare as the cumbersome medieval

Below: A lightly armed Greek warrior.
Bottom: Janissaries were the personal guard of the Ottoman Sultans. Superb soldiers, they were taken from Christian families and converted to the Islamic faith.

Top: The Assyrians were a war-like people. Their empire was built by an aggressive policy of expansion and a superbly equipped and trained army. Assyrian archers wore long coats of mail and were protected by huge rounded shields.
Right: A stone carving of a Viking warrior carrying a heavy round shield and mounted on a horse.

weapons and armour became obsolete.

Fire power did not immediately change traditional military methods: armies still marched to meet the enemy, made camp, and perhaps the next day engaged the enemy in battle. Early firearms had certain limitations; they could not be used in bad weather and so armies continued to go into winter quarters, fighting only in spring, summer, and autumn. The tradition was broken by Napoleon, who introduced speed and mobility into warfare by combining marching, battle, and pursuit into one overall manoeuvre.

Improved technology

Increase in fire power and technological advances during the 19th century forced armies off the battlefield and produced

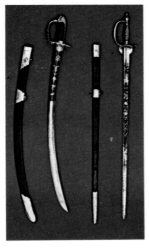

Above: British officers' swords of the Napoleonic era. The sword is one of the oldest of all weapons.

tactics were broken in the Second World War by Germany's use of shock tactics – swift penetration of the enemy lines with armour, mobile infantry, and aircraft.

The dropping of atomic bombs on Japan at the end of the Second World War ushered in the age of nuclear weapons far too powerful to use. So despite the nuclear strength of the great powers conflicts since 1945 have been fought with conventional weapons and in many cases with guerrilla tactics. Conventional military success is no longer so important; revolutionary armies can absorb military defeat and still win in the end.

Below: Modern soldiers, such as these Americans in Vietnam, are specially equipped to fight in difficult areas. Bottom: The M-107 is a 175mm self-propelled gun widely used by NATO armies.

the extended front. The coming of the railways made it possible to move huge armies quickly to the front; instead of individual battles so-called 'theatres of war' developed. The telegraph, too, changed military methods, for commanders could now control their campaigns from headquarters hundreds of miles from the front. The new lessons in warfare were learned at great cost: appalling casualties were suffered in such conflicts as the American Civil War (1861 to 1865), when traditional cavalry and infantry charges were mowed down by enemy fire.

Developments in warfare in the 19th century culminated in the deadlock of the First World War. What was to have been a war of movement developed into a four-year standstill, with opposing forces entrenched in the mud. These defensive

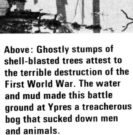

Above: Ghostly stumps of shell-blasted trees attest to the terrible destruction of the First World War. The water and mud made this battle ground at Ypres a treacherous bog that sucked down men and animals.

The Earliest Armies

spears, but used them to stab, like a long dagger. Spears usually had flint heads, but those carried by nobles were made of copper or ivory. Soldiers sometimes carried short battle-axes and wore daggers at their belts. These were usually flint or copper, with wood or bone handles. But the most common Egyptian weapon was the mace, of which there were two types. One was heavy and pear-shaped, capable of cracking an enemy's skull; the other was lighter but had a sharp disc edge.

The Egyptians made up for their infantry's lack of mobility by introducing light chariots drawn by small, fast ponies. They were organized into manoeuvrable groups of 25 which could gallop full speed at the enemy. They operated as a unit, never allowing themselves to be singled

The Egyptians were excellent archers. Their training included loosing arrows from a chariot at full gallop. Foot archers carried a quiver of 30 arrows which they could deliver with deadly effect.

Ancient Egypt and Assyria produced the first organized and trained armies. They also set the pattern for centuries of classical warfare.

Top: The military organization of the ancient Egyptians was highly developed. The main weapon of infantry forces was the spear, though axes and long swords were also common during the Middle Kingdom (2375–1580 BC).

Assyrian armies were reinforced with slingmen among the ranks of infantry. Stationed behind the archers, slingers lobbed volleys of missiles in high arcs. Slingers also carried swords against sudden attack.

The powerful empire of ancient Egypt was formed after the tiny warrior kingdoms along the Nile Valley were united by conquest into two larger kingdoms – Upper and Lower Egypt. The kings of Upper Egypt eventually conquered Lower Egypt and so united the whole valley. As the country became unified so the tribal armies became increasingly organized to defend the empire. From the 18th dynasty (1555 to 1350 BC) onwards, large conscript armies were raised in war to supplement peacetime units such as the pharaoh's bodyguard and the Nubian and Libyan archers. The later pharaohs could raise five divisions of 10,000 men each. These often included enemy captives.

Fighting weapons
Egyptians believed in fighting light, so they wore very little protection. Armour – except for helmets – was almost unknown. Foot soldiers might carry a shield made of hide. Archers were armed with a three-foot bow which shot arrows made of reed with heads of agate or flint, and later copper. Spearmen did not throw their

out and surrounded in battle. The typical chariot had a thin wooden floor with wicker sides and a light rail in front. The driver carried a shield to protect the warrior, who was equipped with a javelin, dagger, bow, mace, and battle-axe.

Cities of blood
'Cursed be the city of blood, full of lies and full of violence. The sound of the whip is heard, the gallop of horses, the rolling of chariots. . . . An infinity of dead, the dead are everywhere.'

So reads the biblical description of the ancient Assyrian capital of Nineveh. In 1000 BC Assyria was the most powerful nation in the Middle East, and by the 8th century BC King Tiglathpileser III had created a large trained standing army of chariots, light cavalry, and infantry, armed with weapons of forged iron. Again the Bible paints a vivid picture of the warlike Assyrians, organized into efficient units of 1000 and 10,000: 'Their roar is that of young lions. . . . None of them will tire, nor will they stumble, none shall stop nor sleep. . . .'

Like the Egyptians, the Assyrians relied heavily on chariots in battle. But the Assyrian chariots were heavier than those of Egypt, with strong wooden sides decorated with paint and metal fittings. They were drawn by two or four horses and carried a driver, a soldier with bow and javelin, and a protecting shield bearer. They were the main strength of an army: in battle, if the ground was suitable, the chariots led by the king acted as a shock weapon.

Heavy infantry included archers, spearmen, and slingmen; the main power rested with the archers who were used in all types of attack. Archers at first wore long coats of mail; later they were protected by large hooded shields.

The Assyrians also equipped a light cavalry, consisting of archers and spearmen. But they were handicapped by having neither saddle nor stirrup, and so could not stand in the saddle to engage the enemy in close fighting.

The Assyrians were rarely beaten. Their empire was almost entirely directed towards military ends and their kings were sound organizers and brilliant commanders. Smaller nations resorted to strong fortifications rather than face the Assyrians in open battle. In response to this the Assyrians developed the art of siege warfare, using techniques that including breaching or scaling walls, tunnelling, and psychological warfare. Archers in mobile towers provided cover for the operators of huge battering rams.

Above: Assyrian chariots were swift, two-wheeled vehicles, each carrying a driver and an archer.

The Assyrians were highly trained in siege tactics. A battering ram hung from a rope inside a mobile turret pounded the walls of towns. Heavily armed soldiers poured through the breach while elsewhere, men with scaling ladders rushed the walls in a number of places. Archers provided continuous covering fire.

An Age of Heroes

During Greece's 'heroic' age battles were fierce trials of strength between warrior heroes; with the conquest of the Greek city states by Philip and Alexander of Macedon the army became a more unified force.

'Let us make ready for battle. Sharpen your spears each man, look to your shields, give the horses a good feed, see that the chariots are prepared – let war be the word! . . . Sweat shall run over many a chest under the strap of his covering shield, many a hand shall tire in grasping the spear!' In these words the Greek poet Homer described the Greek preparations for battle against the Trojans during the 'heroic' age of warfare (2000 to 900 BC). During this period battles were trials of

Right: Ancient Greece was a patchwork of numerous city states which were constantly warring with one another. They united only when a common enemy, such as the Persians, threatened to overrun them all.

Below right: A beautifully decorated Athenian plate portrays the figure of a mythical archer, wearing an unusual close-fitting garment, reaching into his quiver for an arrow.

Below: A Greek urn showing a man and a youth standing in a swift, two-wheeled chariot surrounded by heavily armed hoplites.

GREECE IN THE 5TH CENTURY BC

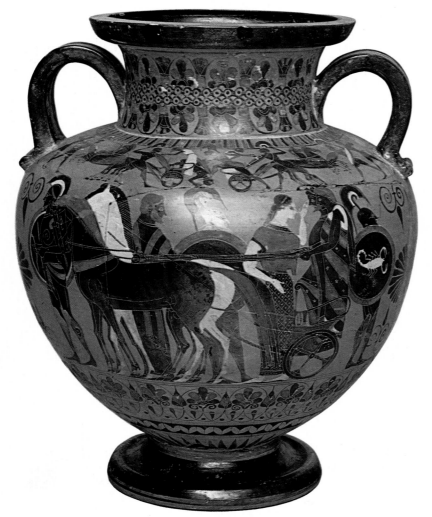

strength and courage between warrior 'heroes'. Soldiers rode on to the field in chariots and dismounted to engage the enemy in single combat. They were lightly armed for agility, carrying a round shield, two throwing spears, and a sword. The bow was considered a cowardly weapon – the spear was always the most important Greek weapon.

The courage of the Spartans

In the 7th century BC Sparta, a city in the southern Peloponnese, became the supreme military state in Greece. Under its ruler, Lycurgus, the entire male population was trained from youth to form a professional standing army, every man abiding by the belief that he must 'conquer or die'. A Spartan soldier fighting in the battle at Thermopylae in 481 BC during the great wars against the Persians was told that the enemy would shoot so many

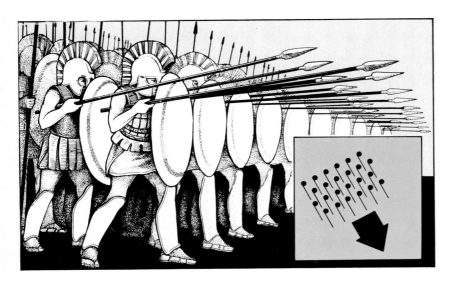

Philip introduced a new type of light infantry, *hypaspists*, who combined the discipline of the trained hoplite with the agility and flexibility of the psiloi. The army now based its success upon a combination of a strong and solid phalanx with light and heavy cavalry providing shock action. Philip also developed the use of siege weapons, such as the catapult and ballista, which his son Alexander the Great was to use not only in sieges, but on the field of battle.

The army that Alexander inherited from his father was without doubt the best trained and equipped and the most powerful of ancient times. With it, this brilliant leader was to make some of the greatest conquests in history.

arrows that they would darken the Sun. 'So much the better,' replied the soldier, 'we shall fight in the shade.'

In battle the Spartan army was organized in phalanxes, a formation which was soon adopted by the other Greek city states. The phalanx was a highly disciplined body of infantry formed in long lines varying from eight to sixteen men in depth. The soldier of the phalanx, the heavily armed hoplite, was well trained and kept fit through constant combat and strenuous exercise in sport.

The hoplites were drawn from the upper and middle classes of free citizens in Greece. Protecting their flanks were *psiloi*, or light troops, drawn from the lower classes, many of whom were mercenaries. These were lightly armed and less well trained and disciplined.

Macedonian cavalry

In the 4th century BC the Greek army was reorganized under Philip of Macedon who, with his son Alexander, conquered the Greek city states. Cavalry was now a superior force, as well trained and equipped as the infantry. The Macedonian cavalryman carried a pike about ten feet long, light enough to be thrown and heavy enough to unhorse his opponent. He also wore a short sword at his belt, carried a shield, and was protected by a breastplate, helmet, and greaves – armour for the lower part of the leg. The horses, too, wore armour headpieces and breastplates.

Philip modified the Greek phalanx to make it more mobile and efficient in battle; the hoplite was now armed with a smaller shield and a 13-foot pike, called a *sarissa*.

In Greece's heroic age, men went into battle in densely packed units known as phalanxes. Each phalanx was an extended rectangle of men that advanced on the enemy behind a wall of bristling spears. This formidable formation – the main weight of any Greek force – was supported by flanking units of lightly armed archers and slingers.

Right: This Etruscan bronze figure wears the armour of a hoplite – the typical soldier of the Greek city state. The hoplite went into battle wearing leg guards (greaves), a metal breastplate and backplate, and a plumed helmet. Greek armies were true citizen forces; all men were required to serve at some time in their lives.

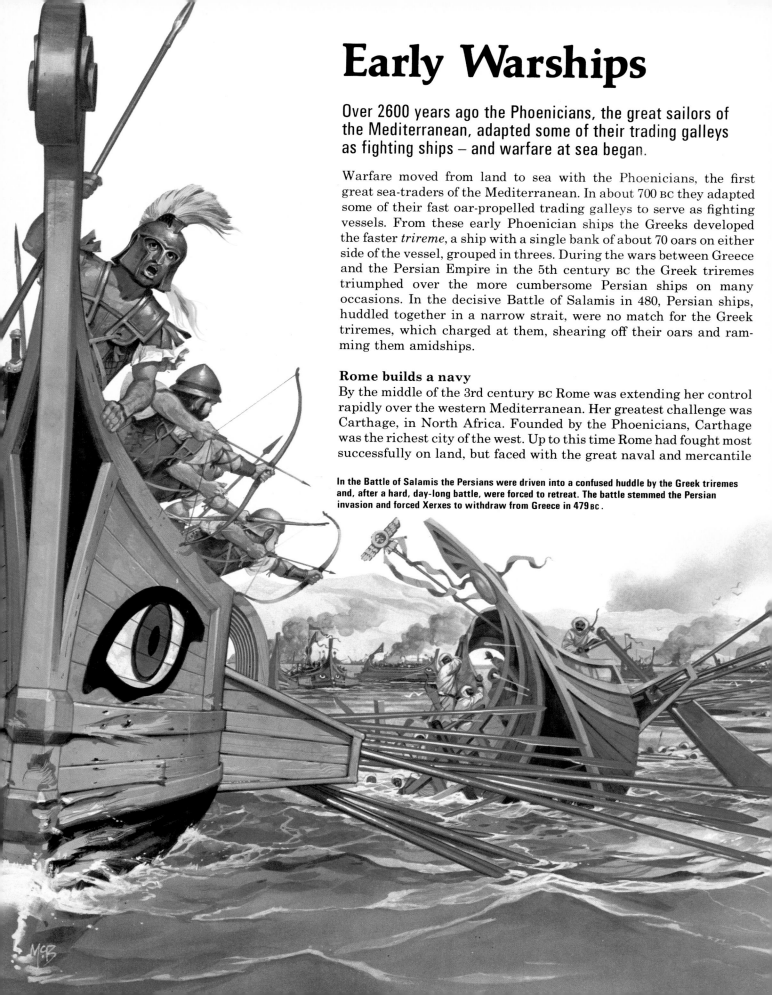

Early Warships

Over 2600 years ago the Phoenicians, the great sailors of the Mediterranean, adapted some of their trading galleys as fighting ships – and warfare at sea began.

Warfare moved from land to sea with the Phoenicians, the first great sea-traders of the Mediterranean. In about 700 BC they adapted some of their fast oar-propelled trading galleys to serve as fighting vessels. From these early Phoenician ships the Greeks developed the faster *trireme*, a ship with a single bank of about 70 oars on either side of the vessel, grouped in threes. During the wars between Greece and the Persian Empire in the 5th century BC the Greek triremes triumphed over the more cumbersome Persian ships on many occasions. In the decisive Battle of Salamis in 480, Persian ships, huddled together in a narrow strait, were no match for the Greek triremes, which charged at them, shearing off their oars and ramming them amidships.

Rome builds a navy

By the middle of the 3rd century BC Rome was extending her control rapidly over the western Mediterranean. Her greatest challenge was Carthage, in North Africa. Founded by the Phoenicians, Carthage was the richest city of the west. Up to this time Rome had fought most successfully on land, but faced with the great naval and mercantile

In the Battle of Salamis the Persians were driven into a confused huddle by the Greek triremes and, after a hard, day-long battle, were forced to retreat. The battle stemmed the Persian invasion and forced Xerxes to withdraw from Greece in 479 BC.

power of Carthage the Romans were forced to build a proper fleet. They did this by improving upon the design of Carthaginian ships – using wrecks as models. In addition to biremes (ships with two banks of oars on either side) and triremes they developed the quinquireme, which carried 100 soldiers and was propelled by 300 oarsmen. The Romans invented a type of drawbridge, known as a *corvus*, for boarding enemy ships. The corvus was hinged to the deck of the Roman ship and lowered on to the deck of an enemy vessel. A long iron spike on its underside pierced the deck of the opposing ship to prevent it pulling away.

Backed by her new navy, Rome fought to victory in the First and Second Punic Wars against Carthage. But with no rivals in the Mediterranean for 600 years after the Punic Wars, the Roman navy was allowed to stagnate. When the barbarian invasions reached the coasts of the Empire in the 3rd century AD, the Roman fleet was powerless against them. In Constantinople, capital of the Eastern Roman or Byzantine Empire a law was passed – too late to have any effect – forbidding the teaching of shipbuilding to the barbarians.

The Byzantine Empire survived the barbarian invasions which had wrecked the Western Roman Empire, but new threats were to come. In 622 the Prophet Muhammad, the founder of Islam, began the expansion of the Muslim empire in the Middle East and North Africa. Faced with the Muslim menace, the Byzantine Empire strengthened its navy. As well as small ships developed along the lines of the Roman bireme they built larger vessels with turrets at either end, equipped with catapults. About AD 670 the Byzantines perfected a secret weapon; the exact composition of it is still unknown. Called 'Greek fire', it was highly combustible and could not be extinguished with water. Tubes mounted in the ships' turrets shot this burning substance at enemy ships, engulfing them with flames.

Seafarers of the North
By the 9th century the greatest threat to Europe came from the seafaring Vikings of Scandinavia. Broad-hulled, strong-keeled boats carried these fierce warriors as far away as Sicily and Russia, but the vessels were of little use in sea combat.

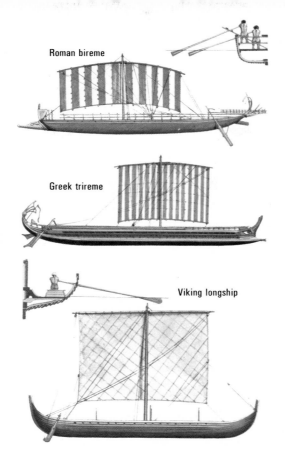

Roman bireme

Greek trireme

Viking longship

Biremes (left) were Roman galleys which had either a double bank of rowers or two rowers to each oar. The Greek trireme (centre) measured up to 140 feet long and weighed 50 tons. A team of 144 galley slaves rowed from cramped positions in the hold, often chained to their benches. Though small and open decked, Viking longships (bottom) were incredibly seaworthy. They were usually propelled by oars unless there was a following wind when a square mainsail could be hoisted. In these frail craft, Vikings criss-crossed the stormy North Atlantic and swept along the coasts of Europe.

They were instead effective vehicles for lightning raids on coastal towns and villages. The shallow draught of the Viking ships enabled them to sail into bays and rivers where other ships would run aground. Surprise was essential to Viking operations, and once the raid had been completed they could make their escape before their victims could retaliate.

During the invasions of England by the Viking Danes, the English King Alfred took the bold step of building up fleets of ships to intercept the raiders at sea. He had more success in defeating the Vikings at sea than on land. The Anglo-Saxon Chronicle records one of Alfred's victories in the summer of 875, when 'he went out to sea with a naval force, and fought against the crews of seven ships, and captured one ship and put the rest to flight'.

The art of naval warfare changed little in the 1500 years between the Phoenicians and the Vikings. Fighting at sea was largely a matter either of destroying enemy ships by ramming or fire, or boarding them to fight what amounted to small-scale land battles. It was not until the introduction of gunpowder that naval warfare developed as a separate art.

A stone monument from Jutland depicting the exploits of a group of Viking marauders. Small bands of lightly armed Vikings pillaged and terrorized the coastal towns of Western Europe during the 9th to 11th centuries. They plundered and disappeared again in their swift ships long before help could be summoned.

The Might of Rome

The Romans, brilliant organizers, created the most successful military force in the ancient world.

The backbone of the great power of Imperial Rome was its army, the first full-time professional army in the world. The security and extent of the vast Roman Empire depended upon its superior military force. Efficiently run, the army survived lapses of discipline and organization and was a united force for 700 years.

The emergence of the legion
In the 5th century BC the Roman army still fought in phalanx formation, its heavily-armed infantry using conventional hoplite tactics. Following a disastrous defeat in 390 BC, the Roman soldier and statesman Marcus Furius Camillus re-fortified Rome and reorganized the army. The phalanx was replaced by the

legion, made up of about 5000 men.

Armies on the march moved in long columns. When advancing into enemy territory, at the end of each day's march the legion built itself a camp in which to spend the night, surrounded by a small ditch and bank with a palisade to keep out wild animals. Sentries gave warning of any approach by the enemy.

Consolidation of the Empire
The Roman Empire reached its greatest extent in the reign of Trajan (AD 98 to 117). As its frontiers were stabilized, defence garrisons were posted all along the borders to defend the Empire from invasion. The Empire's frontier systems included watch-towers from which an eye could be kept on potential invaders. The traditional Roman camp became more elaborate and permanent, developing into the playing-card shaped fort of the 1st century AD. The fort was surrounded by a ditch.

Siege warfare
The Romans were skilled at siege warfare. When all natural means, such as cutting

Every Roman legion carried a standard, a long pole topped by an eagle. On the pole were decorations commemorating past campaigns and victories.

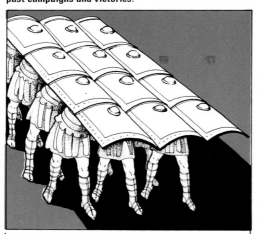

THE TESTUDO
The Roman *testudo* or tortoise formation was a magnificent defensive tactic to protect troops from heavy fire while they advanced towards the enemy line or to the base of a fortress wall. Soldiers interlocked their shields to make a continuous 'roof' of armour under which they could shelter. A well formed testudo was reputed to be able to support the weight of a chariot, its driver, and two horses.

A typical Roman camp was sited near a river. Its perimeter was defended by a ditch, earthen ramparts and wooden palisades. Each wall of the camp had a single gate positioned behind a protective wall. Watchtowers were erected on nearby hills. The camp itself was laid out in a neatly rectangular grid with separate tents for officers, men, and stores. Such camps were a legion's base of operations.

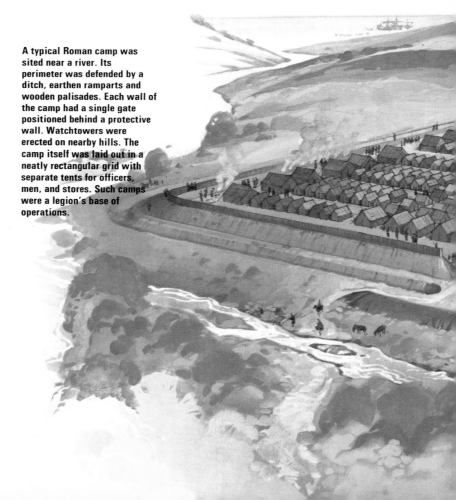

off a town's water supply, had been exhausted, the Romans bombarded and besieged the inhabitants into submission. Ditches were filled to allow access to walls; sometimes huge earth ramps were built to the height of the ramparts so that the attackers could get over the walls. At the same time soldiers protected by mobile sheds worked with iron tools and weapons to undermine the walls. Huge wooden siege towers gave covering fire – some even had drawbridges which could be lowered on to the enemy ramparts. Siege machines such as onagers and spring-guns hurled boulders and iron bolts at the defenders.

The army was responsible for the building and upkeep of roads and bridges all over the Empire, which were fundamental to military communication and manoeuvres. Many civil engineering works were built by the army; most civil projects were designed by army engineers. Though built originally for military purposes, the vast network of roads were vital in holding the Empire together.

From about AD 250, in the face of

The Roman legionary was a well disciplined, highly trained foot soldier. He wore a metal helmet, shoulder guards, body armour, a leather apron and shin-guards.

increased hostility from barbarians, great changes occurred in the structure of the Roman army. The disintegration of the army after about 350 was a symptom of the political and social unrest within the Empire, which was weakened and finally destroyed by the barbarian invasions in the 4th and 5th centuries.

The Romans had built up the most brilliantly organized and successful military force in the ancient world – it was not until the late 19th century that armies would surpass it in competence.

THE LEGION
The main fighting force of the legion in the 4th century BC was divided into three lines: in front were the *hastati* and *principes*, each protected by a helmet, breastplate, and a semi-cylindrical rectangular shield, and armed with two javelins (*pila*), a dagger, and a two-foot double-edged sword (*gladius*). They were backed up by the *triarii*, older men who were similarly armed but carried a thrusting spear instead of a javelin. Each of these groups was divided into ten companies called *maniples*. The heavy infantry were supported by the *velite*, lightly-armed skirmishers, and by cavalry, used for scouting and pursuit.

Roman armies were supported by brilliant engineers. They could erect trestle or pontoon bridges in a matter of hours, across which troops, horses, and carts could be moved.

trestle

pontoon

Warriors of the East

Warfare in Asia developed independently from that in Europe with little contact between the two until Alexander the Great reached India in the 4th century BC.

The Chinese, by tradition, are not an aggressive people. The wars they have fought have been either to repel invaders or 'civil wars' between semi-independent feudal states. China was transformed from a feudal society into a unified nation in 249 BC by Shih Huang Ti, the first of the Ch'in emperors. A tireless builder, he began the construction of the Great Wall of China which stretched for 2000 miles along the northern frontiers of the country to keep out invading tribes.

Early Chinese armies had used chariots in their main force. Under the Ch'in dynasty the Chinese developed the art of siege warfare, using catapults and scaling ladders, some of which were extendable. Fire rockets launched at the enemy were another ingenious weapon.

After centuries of resistance against outside invaders, in the 13th century China was finally conquered by the Mongols, fierce nomadic warriors from the steppes of Central Asia. These expert horsemen moved in vast armies and subdued their enemies by a combination of speed and surprise. The inhabitants of towns and villages overrun by the Mongols were sometimes massacred. Mongol warriors were highly disciplined cavalry, effective as an army when united by a leader such as Genghis Khan and Timur.

Above: A Chinese tomb rubbing from the Han Dynasty (200 BC to 200 AD) depicts a mounted archer loosing his arrows at full gallop.

The samurai

Unlike the Chinese, the Japanese developed a militaristic society which valued the qualities of a good warrior. They evolved a strict code of loyalty and discipline which reached its height with the emergence of the *samurai* in the 12th century AD. Power in Japan during the medieval period was in the hands of feudal landowners who built strong fortified castles and kept their own armies. The samurai belonged to a privileged class. His chief weapons were a bow of

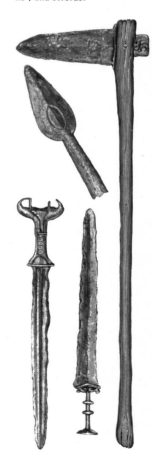

Below: Early Chinese weapons included bronze-headed spears known as 'mau', halberds or 'ko', and swords.

A samurai warrior, a fearsome sight in his splendid armour, which was both protective and decorative.

The Japanese castle of Himeji was as impregnable as the finest fortresses of the Middle Ages in Europe.

boxwood or bamboo and a single-edged sword that had a hard steel edge for cutting but a soft iron core enabling it to withstand blows. Protective armour was made of iron and leather held together with silk or leather cords.

Feudal battles were almost ceremonial, a series of individual duels accompanied by chants, flag signals, drums, and gongs.

In the 16th century the first Europeans reached Japan, bringing with them guns and gunpowder. The Japanese, unlike the Chinese, were eager to learn about these new weapons and quickly adopted them for use in their armies.

The Indian Subcontinent

When Alexander the Great invaded India in 327 BC he faced armies equipped with thundering lines of armoured elephants, driven forward to the accompaniment of shouts and trumpetings. Elephants were an important weapon in the Indian armies until the introduction of firearms in the 16th century. Though an impressive and often terrifying sight to the enemy, elephants were not easily trained, and could be stampeded back into their own ranks with disastrous results. At best they drove holes through the enemy's ranks through which more lightly equipped troops could pour.

The soldiers of ancient India were drawn from a warrior class – the *Ksatriya* – whose status was second only to the priestly class of *Brahman*. The king himself was a member of the Ksatriya and he set the example of skill at arms and sports for the other members. Foot soldiers carried bows of varying lengths made of metal, horn, and wood. Swords were developed to a high degree – by the 15th and 16th centuries AD they were forged of many layers of metal for strength, their hilts inlaid with jewels.

The early Hindu armies were not lacking in courage, but their dependence on elephants, bad organization, and lack of tactical sense weakened them and left them vulnerable against the Islamic invasions of India from the 10th century AD onwards. Firearms were first seen in northern India when Babur the Tiger descended upon India from Samarkand in 1525. Babur laid the basis for the magnificent Moghul Empire which was consolidated by his grandson Akbar.

The siege of a fortress in India by Akbar, the general who consolidated the Moghul Empire in India in the 16th century. Using massive siege cannon and muskets, Akbar swept aside Hindu resistance with ease.

Below: Indian weapons of the 17th and 18th centuries ranged from modern muskets to the more traditional decorated helmets, long, curved swords, elaborate daggers, and the wicked-looking Maru, a double-bladed, curved knife.

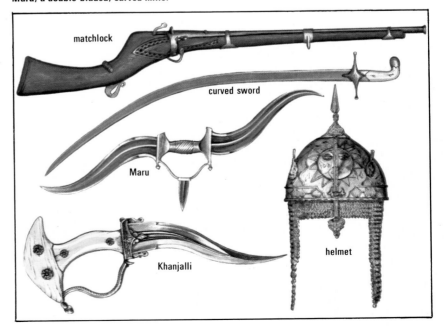

matchlock

curved sword

Maru

Khanjalli

helmet

The Age of Chivalry

Warfare in the Middle Ages was closely tied to the feudal system and its ideals of chivalry.

The most colourful figure of the Middle Ages was the knight, clad in armour from head to foot and mounted on a sturdy charger. Oddly enough it was the introduction in Europe of a seemingly insignificant item – the stirrup – in about AD 700 that revolutionized warfare and established the prowess of the mounted warrior. For the first time a soldier on horseback could stand in the saddle to exchange blows with his enemy or could keep his balance while charging with a lowered lance.

By the 14th century, armour was a mixture of mail and iron plate. A memorial brass of a Belgian knight of this era shows him fully dressed for battle.

The battle fought by the French King Charles the Bold (840–877) at Fontenoy in 841. The armour and weapons shown are actually those of the 14th century, when the illustration was made. Charles decreed that all men who owned horses must be ready to fight. Military service of this kind established the basis of feudalism.

Above: Their lances broken in the first stage of a tournament, two heavily-armoured knights fight on with swords, watched by admiring spectators.

> **HERALDRY**
> To distinguish themselves from their foes on the field of battle medieval knights had bold symbols emblazoned on their shields, horse trappings, and banners. These symbols formed the origins of heraldry, according to which every monarch and knight bore his own 'coat-of-arms'. Heraldic devices came to be used not only in battle, but also upon personal seals and decorations, and were displayed by knights in tournaments and at jousts. They began as personal symbols but later became hereditary so that certain combinations of symbols became associated with particular noble families. Later, when heraldry had lost its practical purpose, it was maintained as a form of embellishment and social distinction.

Feudal warfare

Warfare in the Middle Ages was closely bound up with the feudal system, which first emerged in France under the Emperor Charlemagne in the 8th century. In a feudal society a great lord or king divided his lands among his chief followers – his vassals – who in return swore an oath of loyalty and service to him. Each vassal was bound to raise an army from his estates to fight for the king, usually for a specified length of time each year. It was basically a system of protection in very dangerous times: the less powerful were only too glad to accept the duties exacted by a fighting lord who protected them.

The crack troops serving under a lord were his mounted knights who moved like small armoured tanks around the field of

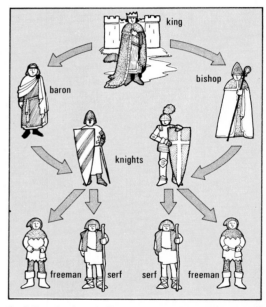

Feudalism dominated all aspects of medieval life. Powerful lords and bishops pledged their allegiance to the king in return for the privileges of land ownership. Knights pledged similar allegiance to their lords. At the bottom of the ladder were the freemen and serfs who farmed the land and worked as craftsmen.

battle, cutting down enemy infantry with crushing blows from their great heavy swords. Knighthood became a matter of great privilege, and eventually much more was expected of a knight than just military service. A code of chivalry developed which not only dictated how he should be trained and armed but also required spiritual preparation for the honour of knighthood. The qualities of courage, honour, and Christian behaviour were placed uppermost in an age of great violence and lawlessness. Ideal qualities of chivalry appear in the character of the Knight in Chaucer's *Canterbury Tales:*

. . . a most distinguished man
Who from the day on which he first began
To ride abroad had followed chivalry,
Truth, honour, generousness and courtesy.

Knights kept fit for fighting by taking part in hunting and hawking parties. But a sport closer still to warfare itself was jousting, friendly but dangerous mock battles staged between famous knights before hundreds of spectators. Tournaments and jousts were often held at the courts of nobles amid colourful pageantry and splendid trappings. In the early days of tournaments the contestants were often maimed and sometimes killed; later jousts were artificially but elaborately staged purely for court entertainment.

Professional armies

The mounted and armoured knights only kept their position of honour and privilege as long as they were the most powerful and efficient soldiers on the battlefield. With the development of first the longbow and then firearms, both of which could penetrate even the strongest plate armour, the power of the knight began to wane. In the Battle of Crécy in 1346 during the Hundred Years' War the French knights were easily brought down by the rain of arrows released from the English longbows. The same war produced a new breed of soldier far removed from Chaucer's 'perfect gentle knight': the mercenary, hired for his fighting skill alone, irrespective of his nationality or social class. As the feudal system began to break down, so it became increasingly necessary to abandon traditional methods of recruitment. Armies became more and more professional, hired to serve on campaigns all the year round.

Above: The coat-of-arms of John de Dreux, Duke of Brittany and Earl of Richmond, showing the elaborate symbols of heraldry.

Below: Knights jousting, from a manuscript of about 1480. The artist has paid more attention to the accuracy of the heraldry on the riders' surcoats and their horses' trappers than to the armour, but he shows the blunt lance-head used in sport, the vamplate on the lance to protect the hand, and the heavy jousting helm.

Knights and Castles

Siege warfare gained new prominence in the Middle Ages with the development of massive castles.

'When the King of England arrived in front of Calais,' wrote one medieval chronicler,. 'he besieged it in the grand manner, and had a mansion and a neat row of houses constructed as if he had come to stay for ten to twelve years. . . . Trade was carried on in his new city, and a market held three times a week.'

Castles and sieges

During the Middle Ages the siege was an important part of warfare, for the strength of the feudal system was founded on the castle, the centre of feudal society. It afforded protection not only to the lord who occupied it, but, in times of siege, to the tenants from his estates.

The earliest medieval fortification was the Norman motte and bailey castle. The motte was a mound surrounded by a ditch; on top of the mound was a wooden stockade with a square wood or stone tower called the keep which was the strongest part of the castle. The bailey was another area enclosed by a stockade, originally for animals. Gradually wooden stockades were replaced by more durable stone, and the keeps became rounded so that they would deflect missiles. Towers were incorporated in surrounding 'curtain' walls for extra fortification.

Castles gradually became larger and more elaborate, especially after the Crusaders saw and copied the magnificent fortresses they found in the Middle East. Castles built by the Crusaders still stand in Syria, Turkey, and the Lebanon.

Despite the development of heavily fortified castles the techniques of siege warfare differed little from those used in ancient times. Walls were approached in wheeled galleries or movable towers with

A variety of tactics and siege machinery were needed in an attack on a heavily fortified medieval castle. From giant siege towers wheeled up to the walls armed men rushed the ramparts. Powerful catapults hurled stones against the walls or into the castle to spread confusion. Huge bombards mounted on fixed platforms fired heavy stone shot at the outer walls to make a breach. Archers kept up a steady hail of arrows to force the defenders back from the walls while men with scaling ladders swarmed up to the ramparts.

roofs to protect the heads of the attackers. Siege engines included the *ballista*, a torsion engine which could launch arrows and stones, the *trebuchet*, and the *mangonel*. The trebuchet, a sling with a counter-weight of up to four tons, could hurl missiles of up to 65 pounds. The mangonel was a large catapult powered by twisted rope which was used to hurl anything from rocks to dead human and animal bodies to create plague in a city. Ladders were used to scale walls; tunnels were dug beneath walls to weaken them.

Weapons and armour

The armour worn during the early Middle Ages was mail – composed of

Above: Typical of the great fortified towns of the late Middle Ages is Carcassonne in the south of France.

Left: The Kiz Kalasi in Turkey, one of many castles built by the Crusaders to protect their conquests in the Holy Land.

Above: The defenders of a castle could not rely on the strength of the walls alone. Soldiers on the ramparts kept up a steady barrage of arrows and other missiles on the attackers below. In the foreground above, an archer shoots through a narrow slit in the walls.

interlinked iron rings. Norman knights wore a long shirt of mail, a conical iron helmet, often with a nose guard, and carried a kite-shaped shield. In the 13th century helmets became larger and were specially shaped to deflect blows. Some of them had visors which came down over the face so that the entire head was enclosed in iron. By the beginning of the 14th century knights were wearing plate armour to protect the more vulnerable parts of their bodies; eventually they wore entire suits of plate armour. An elaborate suit of armour might weigh over 100 pounds.

In battle knights relied on the lance as a shock weapon. It was tucked under the arm, carrying the weight of both man and horse into the attack. Battle-axes, daggers and war hammers were also carried by knights. Swords, which were at first short and broad, became longer and more pointed to penetrate mail armour.

Foot soldiers were chiefly archers and pikemen. The Normans used short bows and crossbows; by the 14th century both of these weapons had been surpassed by the Welsh longbow. About six feet long, it was effective at 200 yards. Skilled long-bowmen could shoot up to ten arrows a minute.

Firearms appeared in Europe in the 13th century – first as cannon, then as handguns which were like small cannon attached to a wooden haft. As the power of these new weapons was realized, so the methods of warfare were to change.

Above: An elaborately decorated suit of plate armour. The introduction of firearms spelled the end of plate armour in battle.

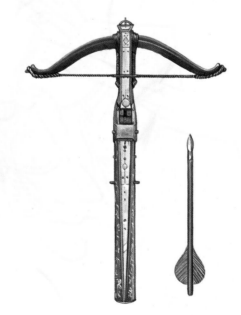

Left: A crossbow and (enlarged) a feathered arrow.

Cannon and Musket

Warfare radically altered after gunpowder was introduced to Europe. The crude medieval cannon is a direct ancestor of the sophisticated firearms of today.

Warfare was revolutionized with the invention of gunpowder. In the West an English monk, Roger Bacon, was the first to record a formula for gunpowder; the first guns appeared in the 14th century.

The earliest handguns were very like simple cannon mounted on long wooden shafts. By the middle of the 15th century the matchlock had been developed. This was fired by a match, a string-like fuse which was brought down to ignite a powder-filled touch-hole, setting off the main charge in the barrel. The presence of lighted matches and exposed gunpowder made this weapon unsafe to load; the flintlock, developed in the 17th century, created a spark only as needed, and was less dangerous. But both the matchlock and flintlock were affected by the weather: armies up to the middle of the 19th century rarely fought on wet days, and hardly ever in the winter. This was eventually overcome by using an explosive cap instead of priming powder.

Until the 19th century most firearms were loaded at the muzzle end, which not only took time but also meant that men had to stand up in front of the enemy to reload. In the 19th century improvements were made in guns that could be loaded at the lock end – breechloaders. At the same time rifling was used more and more in both guns and cannon, increasing range and accuracy. The end of the same century saw the invention of the most important automatic weapon – the Maxim gun.

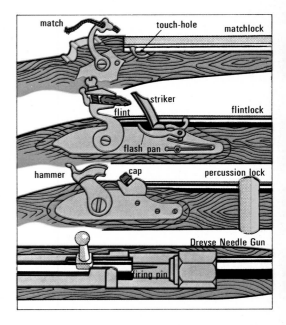

From top to bottom, the lock mechanisms of a matchlock, flintlock, percussion lock, and Dreyse Needle Gun. Early muskets were cumbersome matchlocks that were fired by holding a smouldering fuse to a flash pan, from which a fine trail of powder led to the main chamber and set off the charge. Matchlocks, popular in the 15th and 16th centuries, were eventually replaced by the flintlock. Here, a flint set in the cock flew forward when the trigger was pulled, striking a spark off a steel surface and igniting the priming powder. In the percussion lock gun of the early 19th century, which made priming the gun unnecessary, a high-explosive cap was placed over the touch-hole. In 1837, Johann Dreyse developed the needle gun in which a long needle-like firing pin detonated a cartridge – the forerunner of the modern cartridge rifle.

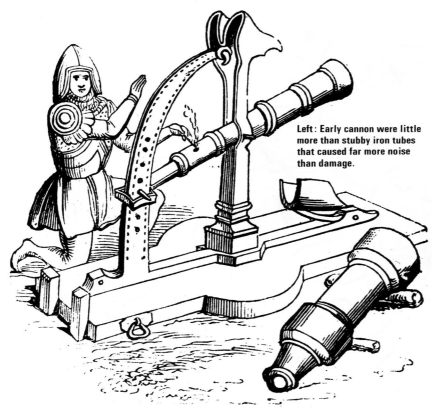

Left: Early cannon were little more than stubby iron tubes that caused far more noise than damage.

Rifling increases the range and accuracy of firearms. By cutting grooves on the inside of a gun barrel it is possible to give the bullet a spin which steadies its course through the air. Like a spinning top, which stays upright, the bullet will hold itself in a straight line by spinning. Rifling was known as early as the 1400s, but not widely used until several hundred years later. A modern bullet (bottom) is a relatively light, hard projectile that is fired at enormous velocities.

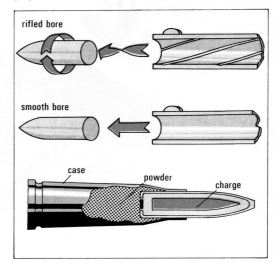

Cannon first appeared in the Middle Ages. By 1700 they could fire anything from a 6-lb to 60-lb ball; the larger cannon were heavy and mounted on cumbersome carriages. Some took up to 16 horses to move: if it rained, they had to be abandoned in the mud. By 1800 cannon were lighter and more manoeuvrable; the most popular sizes were between 3 lb and 18 lb. During the First World War tanks and mechanically propelled carriages were developed. Today, with rockets carrying nuclear, gas, and biological shells, fire power has reached frightening proportions.

Right: The heavy cannon of about 1700 gave way to lighter, more manoeuvrable cannon a century later.

Below: A self-propelled gun is a field gun mounted on a chassis to give increased mobility in combat. The Swedish 155 mm 'Bandkanon' is mounted on a tank chassis and can travel at 17 mph. The gun has a maximum range of 142 miles. A 7·62 mm machine gun protects the crew.

c. 1700

c. 1800

Above: Hiram Maxim with his invention of 1884 – the Maxim gun, the first portable, automatic machine gun. Its rate of fire was so rapid that its barrels had to be water-cooled. The recoil of each firing was used to drive the loading mechanism and fire the next round. The gun continued to fire as long as the trigger was pressed.

Top: The first machine guns were heavy, more like field guns than infantry weapons. The Gatling Gun, invented during the American Civil War, had six to ten barrels that fired in succession. They were turned by a hand crank.

Below: This bronze falconet of 1672 is a superb example of a light field gun of the time.

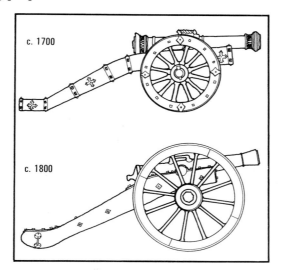

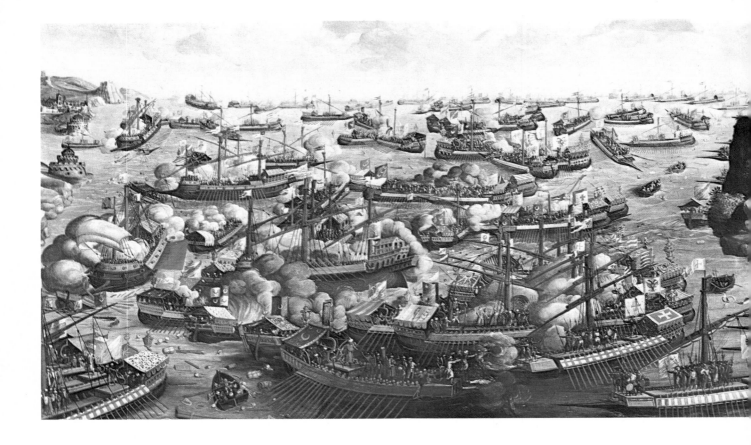

Lepanto and Sea Power

A new kind of naval warfare emerged after the Battle of Lepanto, the last great sea battle fought between oared ships.

As his men prepared for battle at dawn on October 7, 1571, Don John of Austria called for his pipes and danced a galliard in full armour on the deck of his flagship *Real*. He was certain that the combined Spanish and Italian fleet he commanded would shatter the evenly matched Turkish fleet waiting in the Gulf of Lepanto off the Greek coast. Ali Pasha commanded an 'infidel' fleet of 210 galleys, 44 galleots (lighter and swifter version of the galley) and 44 lesser vessels. Opposed to him was a Christian fleet of 202 galleys, 70 frigates, and six galleasses. It was these galleasses in his fleet that gave the Austrian commander such confidence of victory.

Galley-cum-galleon

The galleass was a larger version of the galley and the forerunner of the heavily armed fighting ship of the future, the fully rigged galleon. It combined the manoeuvrability of the oared galley (used for boarding and ramming) with the fire power of the galleon. It had two or three masts to the galley's one, needed fewer oarsmen, and could carry some 30 guns to the galley's maximum of 14. Galleasses were so highly prized that only aristocrats were allowed to command them.

At dawn on October 7 the Turkish fleet left the Bay of Lepanto. As the two fleets sighted each other the Turks deployed into a line abreast formation. The wind filled their painted sails and the green flag of the Prophet streamed from their mastheads. As the Turks swept down on the enemy, the wind suddenly dropped. The Christian fleet deployed. Sails were furled and guns prepared. The Turkish galleys stepped up the rhythm of their oars.

As the Turks passed through the Christian galleasses they were bombarded from above with cannon and raked with musket fire and arrows. There arose all around the

The Battle of Lepanto, in 1571. A Turkish fleet of about 300 ships clashed with a somewhat smaller Christian fleet at the mouth of the Gulf of Lepanto. The two fleets fought in rigid formations: individual ships closed with one another and the soldiers on board engaged in hand-to-hand combat.

Below: A seaman is flogged with the 'cat-o'-nine-tails'. In the 18th century a seaman's life was a hard one, and discipline was often severe.

sounds of war – the crashing of prow against prow, the hiss and thud of arrows, the crackle of arquebuses, the cries of triumph and the screams of death. By afternoon the battle was over. In the three-hour action 53 Turkish galleys had been sunk, 117 had been captured, and many others had been beached on the nearby Greek coast. They left behind them 30,000 dead and 8000 prisoners. The victorious Christian fleet had lost 9000 dead and 13 vessels.

The Battle of Lepanto, which saved Europe for ever from the Turkish threat, was the last great sea battle between oared ships. Henceforward the highly seaworthy and heavily armed galleon was to be the principal fighting ship.

The ships that fought at Lepanto would not have seemed particularly strange to the fighting seamen of the ancient world, who fought in long, sleek, swift ships propelled by banks of oarsmen. The galleys of Lepanto were developed from these single-deck biremes and triremes used in early Mediterranean warfare.

Broadside to broadside

Although Lepanto was the last major battle between warships powered by oars, a number of galleys and galleasses sailed with the Spanish Armada to invade England in 1588. The English galleons which blocked their path came from a new age of sea warfare. Propelled by sail alone these heavily armed ships were, for their day, very large. The guns were positioned below the main deck and were fired broadside through ports in the hull. It was no longer necessary to close with enemy ships and capture them in hand-to-hand combat; they could be destroyed by broadsides of fire.

During the 17th and 18th centuries the French, Dutch, Spanish, and British struggled for control of the oceans. Larger ships were built. The big ships sailed into battle in a line – hence the name 'ships of the line'. The biggest, or first rate, with three decks, could carry over 100 guns; a second rate had 90 to 100 guns; and the third rate carried 70 guns on two decks. Range and accuracy of fire were particularly important as the ships fought broadside to broadside, smashing hulls and masts and killing men until the badly crippled enemy ships either surrendered or sank.

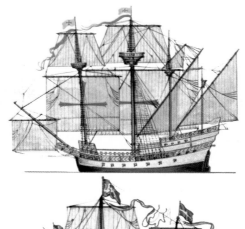

Above, top to bottom: A Spanish galleon, 1550; a Dutch man-of-war, 1613; and an English First Rate, 1780. Spanish galleons of the 16th century replaced the broader and heavier carracks. Their lines were more graceful and they sailed much better. The Dutch man-of-war had three gundecks and could bring a very heavy fire to bear on an enemy ship. An English 'first rate' ship of the late 18th century fired more than 100 guns with its full broadside.

'La Belle Poule' was a powerfully armed 44-gun French frigate built in 1834. One of the largest ships of its type, it was some 210 feet long and on its two gundecks carried cannons firing a 30-pound shot. French frigates of this kind were among the finest sailing ships ever known.

CONDITIONS AT SEA
During the 17th and 18th centuries volunteers for the harsh life aboard a British ship of the line were all too few. Compulsion was needed to man the fighting ships. Many of the crew were convicts sent from prisons. Others were forced into service by press-gangs, armed men who seized mariners from merchant ships and landsmen from ale-houses and harbour streets. Once aboard, the punishment these 'captives' could expect for rebellion was harsh. Food was foul, pay was little and irregular, and health-care almost non-existent. If disease broke out, it spread rapidly through the overcrowded decks and a sailor wounded in action would be lucky to be given rum to ease the pain of an amputated limb.

The New Armies

When the Swedish king Gustavus Adolphus reorganized his armies in the 17th century they became a model for all the countries of Europe.

Gustavus Adolphus, king of Sweden, was a fearless soldier, a brilliant leader, and one of the greatest generals in history. So completely did he revolutionize warfare that he has become known as the father of the modern army.

Gustavus became king at the age of 17 in 1611. At that time Sweden was at war with Denmark, Russia, and Poland. Gustavus saw that the ill-equipped, poorly trained and badly led army he had inherited could never win the important victories needed to realize his ambition of making Sweden the most powerful nation in the Baltic. It would have to be reorganized and retrained.

Modernizing the army

Gustavus set about transforming his army into small, lightly equipped and highly mobile units supported by light and equally mobile artillery. His army was a strictly disciplined force yet punishments, by the standards of the time, were lenient; flogging, for instance, was abolished. Gustavus commanded loyalty by seeing that his troops were properly fed, regularly paid, and warmly clothed. He put his men into uniforms and issued field glasses and maps to his officers. He set an example to other leaders by creating an army that respected civilians and their property; instead of living off the country by pillage and forage his troops were supplied from fixed bases.

The basic infantry of Gustavus's mainly

Above: An Officer of Pikemen of about 1650.
Below: Gustavus Adolphus at the Battle of Breitenfeld, 1631. Swedish victories in the Thirty Years' War marked Sweden's emergence as an important European power.

conscript army was the squadron, which consisted of 192 musketeers and 216 pikemen. His aim was to increase fire power on the field and so he replaced the old matchlock musket with the lighter and more reliable wheel-lock musket. He simplified and speeded up loading by issuing paper cartridges containing powder and shot. The pikemen were used to protect the musketeers while they were reloading; they were also used in attack after the musket volleys had caused confusion in the enemy ranks. Cavalry, charging at full gallop with sabres drawn, would at the same time support the attack.

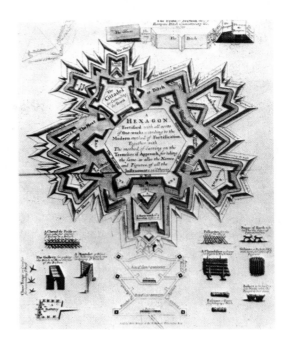

A fortified hexagon showing details of defence. Siege warfare predominated throughout the 17th and much of the 18th centuries. One of the most brilliant practitioners of the art of fortress building was the French engineer Vauban. His squat, massive forts were a virtually impregnable system of stone-faced ditches, slopes (glacis) below the walls that gave clear fields of fire, successive ranks of earthen walls, and large and small projections (bastions) that protected the vulnerable angles of the walls. Forts were built in star-shaped patterns for maximum concentration of fire by the defenders.

SIEGE WARFARE

The most common form of warfare during the 17th and early 18th centuries was the siege of a city or fortress. The French engineer the Marquis de Vauban built or repaired 160 fortresses during his life and he devised rules for both attack and defence. A besieging army would dig lines of trenches (parallels) opposite the section of the wall they had chosen to attack. Zig-zag trenches connected each parallel as they drew nearer the fortress and batteries of cannon were brought up to pound a hole in the walls. If the fortress did not surrender the breach was stormed by the attacking troops. Once they had been surrounded the defenders relied on their cannon and the lines of earth walls around the city to keep the attackers at bay.

Mobile artillery

One of Gustavus's great contributions was in new ways of using artillery. Traditional heavy guns, although effective at the start of an engagement, were far too clumsy to be of any use in a battle of movement. They were soon left behind as the battle moved forward. To give his troops artillery support throughout a battle Gustavus saw that he would have to reduce the weight of his cannons and introduced small, 'regimental' guns that could be moved by one horse or three men. For the first time artillery could be moved over the battlefield as quickly as the infantry.

Mobility and fire power were again Gustavus's objectives in reorganizing troop formations. He discarded the traditional column with the infantry in the centre and the cavalry packed at the wings. Instead, he adopted a chessboard pattern with half his infantry in the centre and the rest dispersed at the wings

in small units between squares of cavalry. This allowed both cavalry and infantry to change direction quickly when necessary. Within the line the artillery were positioned so as to co-ordinate their fire.

The army of Gustavus Adolphus was the first professional standing army; its tactics, weapons, and organization were superior to those of any force of the time. When in 1630 Sweden entered the Thirty Years' War, her victories over the Catholic Habsburg armies saved the cause of Protestantism in Germany. Gustavus was killed in this war in 1632 at Lützen, fighting as always in the thick of the fray.

Swedish infantrymen of the mid-17th century were professional soldiers dressed in standard uniforms and issued with wheel-lock muskets. Guns had by this time become the main weapon of the infantry and were rapidly replacing pikes. These musketeers also carried into battle powder, shot, cartridges, a sword, and a musket rest for their guns.

The Private Soldier

The conditions of army life, often harsh in the past, have been most sharply felt by the private soldier.

For thousands of years, kings, politicians, and dictators have waged wars for religion, for power, or territorial gain. The private soldier who fought and died in these wars often did not know why he was fighting: his job was to obey orders. Some fought voluntarily; others were obliged to serve. Some of those who volunteered were mercenaries, who fought willingly for anyone provided they were paid well for it. Others fought out of religious or patriotic zeal. Still others joined armies to escape hardship at home – or the long arm of the law. In the 18th century recruitment was often a polite word for the trickery that was resorted to in raising armies.

Discipline

From the 16th century soldiers, often a motley crew of rogues and ruffians, were poorly equipped and trained. Discipline, where it existed, was harsh, but often both discipline and training were neglected. But with the growth of standing armies in the 17th century discipline and order became essential, and desertion and cowardice were punishable by death. Lesser offences were punishable by various means including 'running the gauntlet', imprisonment, flogging, and fining men out of their pay (when they got any).

A soldier's life has seldom been easy. Though in the 6th century BC the Persian king Cyrus the Great gave his victorious soldiers 'slaves to wait upon them and to minister to their every need', more often the soldier has been badly fed, poorly dressed, and forced to live in appalling conditions. The 200,000 men of the French army fighting the Prussians in the 1750s consumed 400,000 pounds of mouldy flour each day, supplied through contractors termed 'a league of bloodsuckers'. Food shortages were common. Bread and biscuits, when available, were often maggoty,

Above: Discipline has always been an essential part of running an army. But nothing in the armies of today matches the severity of the punishment once inflicted on men for even the most trivial offences. Flogging at the triangle was all too common in the 18th century. A soldier was tied naked to a rack of upright spears and beaten with a knotted lash called the 'cat-o'-nine-tails'. Punishment for some offences might run to 2000 strokes.
Top: As the scale of military operations grew over the centuries, armies came to depend on a huge supply and transport corps. Armies on the march were slowed to a crawl by their long baggage trains, a host of wives and camp followers, and their ever-reluctant civilian wagon drivers who often refused to bring supplies and ammunition to the field of battle.

Persian spearman
c. 500 BC

14th-century longbowman

Danish guardsman,
Thirty Years' War

and meat was a rarity. Soldiers and sailors on board ship contracted scurvy through the lack of fresh vegetables and fruit; it was not until 1795 that British sailors were issued with limes to combat this disease – hence the term 'limey', eventually applied to all British by the Americans.

Surgery on the battlefield

Until the middle of the 19th century those wounded in battle were subject to the horrors of primitive and insanitary medicine. Flesh wounds were patched up or plastered without being cleaned first; amputation of limbs was often used as a quicker and more expedient way of curing wounds and preventing the spread of gangrene. Amputations were carried out without the use of anaesthetics; the only antiseptic was vinegar, or the binding into wounds of maggots to eat the mouldering flesh. The wounded frequently died, but death often had nothing to do with battle. Insanitary conditions were breeding places for disease, and more soldiers on campaign died from typhus, dysentery, or cholera than were killed on the battlefield. In the 1850s Florence Nightingale introduced sanitation and proper nursing care into hospitals at the front during the Crimean War; in 1863 the Red Cross was founded to provide medical care for the wounded of all sides in war.

The great advances in medicine of the 20th century cut down the number of deaths in warfare dramatically. Despite the appalling number of deaths on both sides during the First World War, the losses would have been multiplied tenfold a hundred years earlier. The development of penicillin early in the Second World War also saved countless lives.

At the Battle of Strasbourg in 1528, a wounded soldier is treated in the field while all around the battle rages. Despite the attendance of a doctor, the chances of surviving a wound were very slender. Medical care was so appallingly primitive – at least until the second half of the 19th century – that untreated wounded soldiers stood the same chance of survival as the treated. Not surprisingly army surgeons were often referred to as 'battlefield butchers' – for they possessed no anaesthetics, few medicines and only the most crude instruments.

Right: A Red Cross ambulance in the field somewhere in Libya during the desert campaign of 1942. The Red Cross was established by international treaty to provide emergency treatment and care for wounded soldiers of all armies. Its humanitarian role is universally respected and it has won unqualified admiration for its work both on and off the battlefield.

Below: The common soldier in each age has often borne the brunt of the fighting and the worst of battlefield conditions. Soldiers were often ill-trained, poorly equipped, and reluctant to fight. Prior to the Thirty Years' War, soldiers were often hired for a limited period and had no great desire to take risks. As army organization became more complex, training improved and the importance of good health and morale was recognized.

Prussian foot soldier, 1750

Russian infantryman, 1812

Confederate private, American Civil War

German machine gunner, 1914–1918

American G.I., 1942

27

Strategy and Tactics

In the last 200 years warfare has become increasingly complex and strategy and tactics have developed as a serious study for military theorists.

A Frenchman once said that 'war is much too serious a thing to be left to military men'. Since the end of the 18th century warfare has become increasingly complex; improvements in weapons, mass production, and the increase in population have all contributed to the growth of total war in which all the resources of a nation, not only its armed forces, are involved in warfare. To cope with this new complexity, new theories of war developed in the 19th century.

Theories of war

The theory and practice of war is divided into strategy and tactics. Strategy is concerned with the formation of alliances and overall war aims; tactics with the movement and conduct of troops in battle.

By the late 18th century warfare had become largely defensive. Armies were not well organized and they were slow on the march. Heavy guns often became bogged down on the poor roads. Frederick the Great, who came to the throne of Prussia in 1740, attempted to alter this. He recommended 'short and lively' wars, and drilled his troops so that they could deploy quickly for battle. He was a strict disciplinarian and expected a great deal from his men. Once, when his troops hesitated before going into a fierce battle, he asked, 'Rascals, do you expect to live for ever?'

The French Revolution which began in 1789 was the first time a nation was involved totally in war. The first citizen army was created and when Napoleon came to power he used it to fight many successful battles by out-manoeuvring the enemy. He split his armies into small units so they could move across country faster, and concentrated them only when he wanted to fight a battle. Each unit was self-contained, with its own cavalry, infantry, and supplies.

Napoleon's conduct of war was studied by the Swiss military theorist Henri Jomini, who laid down rigid principles of warfare; and by Karl von Clausewitz, who stressed the importance of the political aim in warfare, and the role that chance played. Their work was studied by later writers. By this time the spread of railways and improvements in weapons were changing the theory and practice of war. Count Helmuth von Moltke, who became Prussian Chief of Staff in 1858, reorganized the army and used railways to mobilize his troops quickly to concentrate them on the battlefield at Sadowa where he defeated the Austrians in 1866. Many commanders like Moltke came to believe that attack was the only way of fighting. The French commander in the First World War, Marshal Foch, summed it up when he said, 'My centre is giving way, my right is in retreat; situation excellent. I shall attack.'

Defensive warfare

But increased fire power also meant that attacks over open ground could be very costly. The Americans learnt this in the early battles of the Civil War, when the traditional cavalry charge resulted in the wholesale slaughter of men and animals. And as one observer of the

Frederick the Great (1712–1786) made Prussia one of the leading military powers in 18th-century Europe. He trained his troops superbly and organized his army into a highly efficient fighting machine. By introducing light, horsedrawn artillery capable of movement during battle, he was able to direct cannon fire in front of his attacking troops at the decisive moment.

General Helmuth von Moltke was a brilliant military strategist who devised the German offensive that opened the First World War and led the German Army through Belgium and nearly to the gates of Paris.

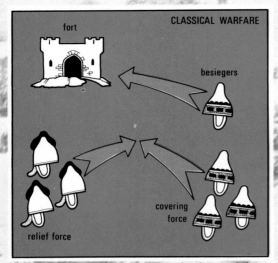

CLASSICAL WARFARE

fort

besiegers

relief force

covering force

Above: Classical warfare often involved a siege carried out by part of the attacking force; the remainder covered them against attack by the enemy's relief force.
Below: Karl von Clausewitz (1780–1831), one of the great military thinkers of all time.

disastrous Charge of the Light Brigade in 1854 during the Crimean War remarked, 'It is magnificent, but it is not war'.

So soldiers dug themselves into the earth, and during the First World War fighting became defensive. Neither the tank nor aircraft succeeded in breaking the stalemate on the Western Front. After the war such military authorities as Sir Basil Liddell Hart suggested new ways to use these weapons. His ideas were developed by the Germans into *Blitzkrieg*, or 'lightning war', which they used successfully against the Poles and the French in 1939 and 1940. The offensive became important once more.

Today the terrifying power of modern nuclear weapons has forced tacticians to rely on fast-moving forces and dispersal on the battle-field. Fortunately these theories have not been tested in practice. The world has also seen the development of guerrilla warfare in which small groups of insurgents attempt to undermine the government from within through individual acts of terrorism.

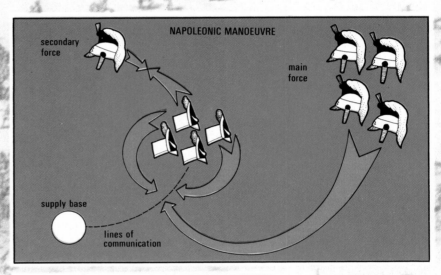

NAPOLEONIC MANOEUVRE

secondary force

main force

supply base

lines of communication

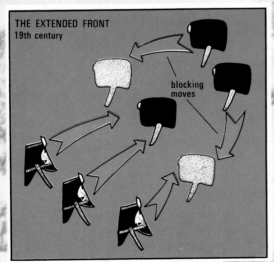

THE EXTENDED FRONT
19th century

blocking moves

Above: The extended front was a natural outcome of the chess-like positioning moves that initiated battles in the 19th century. Each army tried to block the enemy from obtaining a tactical advantage by matching every move with a countermove. This led in the end to huge forces manoeuvring on an ever extending front that finally became the continuous front of the First World War.

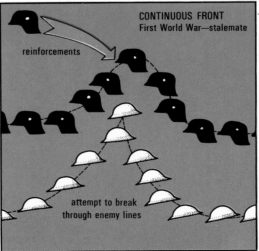

CONTINUOUS FRONT
First World War—stalemate

reinforcements

attempt to break through enemy lines

Above: The rapid extension of fronts during the 19th century produced the continuous fronts of the First World War. These fronts demanded defensive rather than offensive tactics, as frontal assaults resulted in catastrophic loss of life. Attack at any one point in the line could be repulsed by bringing up reinforcements from farther down the line.

Above: Napoleon specialized in using part of his force to engage the enemy while the main force circled round to attack the enemy's line of communications.

The French Marshal Foch, although a supremely competent commander, was a soldier of the old school who placed his faith in massed infantry charges.

29

The Age of Napoleon

Napoleon, a master strategist, discarded traditional methods of warfare; instead he combined speed, mobility, and a keen sense of timing to make his brilliant conquests.

'Liberty, equality, fraternity!' So cheered the French when their monarchy was overthrown in 1789. Having fought and won the Revolution, the citizens of France did not mind when, under their new leader Napoleon Bonaparte, the order came that all childless men between 18 and 40 were liable for military service. In this way Napoleon raised a huge citizen army – one that was relatively ill-trained, a fact that was to affect Napoleon's tactics throughout his campaigns.

Conscription
Napoleon's army was not the only European army of the day to introduce conscription. Prussia and Spain required military service for three years; Austria-Hungary for five. Russia had such a huge population that only a percentage of its men were needed every year for the army: each village was obliged to produce a set number by drawing lots, or ballots.

For garrison duties and home defence Britain also used a ballot system, but the regular army was made up entirely of volunteers. Many of these volunteers transferred from the local militia into the regular army, where they were regarded as likely to be steadier soldiers than the average recruit. Because of its volunteer status Britain's army was small but very well trained. The soldiers were drilled and drilled in making quick and unconfused manoeuvres – a skill that would pay off when they faced Napoleon's numerically superior forces later on.

A brilliant general
Napoleon was a master of strategy. He combined speed and co-ordination to move his armies to the front. Every move on a campaign was planned well in advance, and Napoleon himself scrutinized every aspect of its organization – weapons, uniforms, supply, and even plans for governing conquered territories.

French strategy and tactics were offensive. The army moved swiftly in small groups in forced marches, living off the land so that they were not encumbered by supply trains. At the point of battle these groups would come together as a con-

Right: Napoleon Bonaparte, a master of strategy, made use of his brilliant sense of timing to gain victory on the battlefield.

Below: Napoleon's use of infantry in densely-packed columns (right) was a spectacular success at first and was imitated by most of his opponents. Only the English continued to employ conventional line formations which were reduced to a depth of only two ranks (left). This 'thin red line' could deliver a thundering volley that shattered infantry columns with a hail of bullets from both the front and the flanks.

centrated force to smash the enemy at its weakest point. Part of Napoleon's success in battle was due to his perfect sense of timing. As he himself said, 'the fate of a battle is a question of a single moment.'

Napoleon's infantry were deployed either in long lines or in densely packed columns which battered the enemy line after it had been weakened by artillery fire and skirmishers.

Defeat

Ironically, some of Napoleon's greatest strengths contributed to his downfall. In 1808 a British expeditionary force landed in Portugal. It was the start of the Peninsular campaign which set in motion the train of events which eventually led to the French defeat.

The small and professional British army was well disciplined and organized. When Sir Arthur Wellesley, later Duke of Wellington, took command in the Peninsula in 1809, he attached great importance to the care and training of his troops. The British always had a firm supply base and a well organized supply line. They paid for local produce, so gaining the support of the native population.

The weakness of the dense French column was that only the first two ranks could fire at any one time. Wellington deployed his troops in long double lines; in doing this he created four times the fire power of his enemy. As the French advanced shouting to boost their courage, Wellington's well disciplined troops stood firm and silent, throwing the French into confusion. When the British musket volleys finally came they swept the French ranks, which broke up in disarray.

In 1810 Wellington decided to retreat to his supply base in Portugal; the French followed him. By winter the British were secure and well supplied; the French were hopelessly far from their bases. They retreated, and Wellington began the long slow push which finally defeated the French in the Peninsula in 1814.

The French retreat from Moscow, 1812. Napoleon's capture of Moscow in 1812 proved to be his most costly 'success' ever. The Tsar refused to admit defeat, and Napoleon was forced to withdraw as the fierce Russian winter set in. His troops suffered appallingly on the long march back as the bitter cold, lack of food and shelter, and constant harrassment by the Russians took their toll.

The French victory over the Austrians at Fleurus in 1794 introduced something new to battlefield tactics. The French made use of a hot air balloon as an observation platform.

Technology in War

Technological advances in the 19th century made the pitched battle obsolete. Instead massive armies spread out over an extended front.

In the years after the Napoleonic Wars, spurred on by the Industrial Revolution and the development of mass production, there was a great improvement in the quality and quantity of manufactured goods. At the same time there was a vast increase in population: in 1800 the population of Europe was 170 million; by 1850 it had risen to 274 million.

Increased fire power
Developments which most affected the way war was waged on land were those in weapons and communications. Breech-loading guns and cannon and rifled barrels,

in widespread use by the middle of the century, increased the speed of fire and accuracy on the battlefield. Improved accuracy and later the introduction of automatic weapons forced tactics to change, for traditional methods of fighting produced terrible casualties. No longer could opposing troops line up in brightly coloured uniforms in full sight of each other; with the new fire power they were sitting ducks. Instead soldiers were spread out loosely over an extended front. If a halt was called they dug themselves in, 'burying' themselves, as someone observed, in order to live. This was the beginning of the trench warfare which reached a complete stalemate in 1914.

Right: A hot-air balloon of about 1860. The development of balloon technology improved their reliability as reconnaissance craft. By the middle of the 19th century, they were becoming widely used in battle to direct the fire of artillery batteries, to spot troop movements and the arrival of reinforcements, and to co-ordinate the deployment of troops.

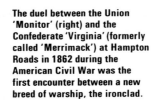

The duel between the Union 'Monitor' (right) and the Confederate 'Virginia' (formerly called 'Merrimack') at Hampton Roads in 1862 during the American Civil War was the first encounter between a new breed of warship, the ironclad.

At the same time uniforms became more loose-fitting and practical – they were made in drab colours that blended better with the landscape, providing protection through camouflage.

Railways and telegraph
With the spread of the rail network troops could be moved rapidly from one front to another. Battlefields no longer had set limits and surprise attacks became easier to carry out. But railways were easy targets for sabotage: lines passed through remote areas where they could not be protected. The destruction of a railway bridge or a portion of the line could immobilize an army.

A short railway was used as a supply route by the British in the Crimea (1854 to 1855), but the first war in which railways were used on a large scale was the American Civil War (1861 to 1865). There the battle front stretched for thousands of miles from the Mississippi River to the Atlantic, and supply bases were often far behind the lines. Roads were few and inadequate, but the railway lines reached out almost as far as the frontiersmen had penetrated.

In Europe the importance of a strong rail link was realized by the Prussian Chief of Staff, Count Helmuth von Moltke. In most European countries the rail network developed in a relatively haphazard way according to the needs of business and the whims of landowners. But in Prussia the system was carefully planned

A Krupps munitions factory in Germany in 1914. The development of mass production in the 19th century meant that by the outbreak of the First World War weapons and equipment could be produced on a scale never before envisaged.

so that huge army reserves could be quickly mobilized on any section of border that might be under attack.

Co-ordination of these huge armies would have been impossible without a very important invention – the telegraph. Besides giving military commanders control over armies that might be hundreds of miles away, it permitted politicians to keep a close eye on their generals, some-thing which was not always welcomed by the military. During the American Civil War, President Lincoln was able to issue daily orders to his generals in the field. That war demonstrated another disad-vantage of the telegraph. On a Confederate raid into Union territory telegraph lines were tapped and false orders were trans-mitted to the enemy, causing havoc when troops were sent off in the wrong direction.

The troops used in this raid were an example of the successful merging of the old and new methods of warfare. They were literally mounted infantry, carrying the latest in repeating rifles and revolvers and riding to war on horseback. They had both mobility and fire power; their method was to hit hard and then disappear. These men, like their counterparts, the Dutch settlers, or Boers, in the South African War fought 40 years later, were the natural soldiers in a country where riding and shooting were everyday skills.

RAILWAYS
Railways and the telegraph transformed mobility and control of land forces in warfare. The importance of artillery grew rapidly. In the American Civil War heavy siege mortars were transported on different types of flat railway wagon (right). Timber trestle bridges which could be rapidly assembled from heavy balks 12 inches square or over, were used during the American Civil War and the South African War.

The First World War

Hopes for a quick victory in the First World War faded as both sides were forced to halt and dig in on a front line that hardly shifted over the next four years.

In August 1914 the 'Great War' broke out – a war which involved almost every country in Europe. The war reflected the mood of the people and was immediately popular. As the troops left for the battlefields they were feted and their weapons decorated with flowers. 'We'll be home by Christmas!' was the soldiers' parting cry. The generals, too, expected a quick end to the war. They planned for a swift mobilization of their armies and a decisive all-out attack to gain victory in a few months.

The reality
Following the traditional pattern of European wars, the soldiers attacked in large groups without using cover or camouflage, trying to overrun the enemy by sheer weight of numbers in hand-to-hand combat. But modern weapons, particularly the machine gun, made such tactics very costly: in one day, for instance, the British lost 20,000 men.

The scope of the war began to spread. In October 1914 Turkey entered the war on the side of the Central Powers; in March 1915 Italy joined the war of attrition engaging the Austrians in a front line that stretched along the Alps. On the Eastern Front the out-numbered but efficient German forces clashed with the ill-equipped

Above: A French soldier (foreground) and British soldiers in a front-line trench in 1916.

Below: Developments in technology produced a range of new weapons and equipment for use during the First World War, the first truly mechanized war.

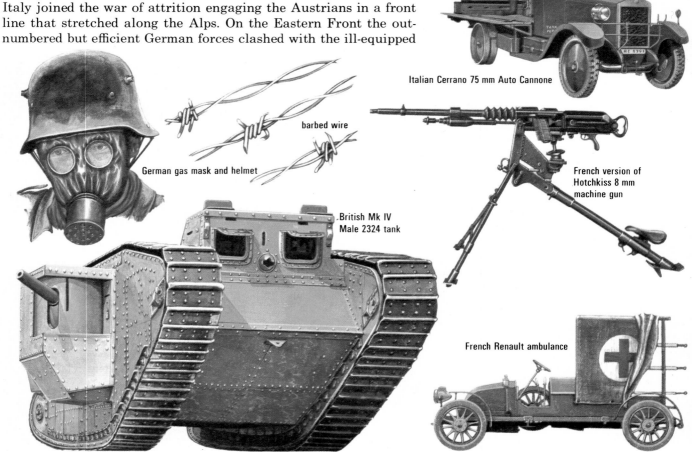

Italian Cerrano 75 mm Auto Cannone

barbed wire

German gas mask and helmet

British Mk IV Male 2324 tank

French version of Hotchkiss 8 mm machine gun

French Renault ambulance

and badly led armies of Tsarist Russia. The result was disastrous: at the Battle of Tannenberg in August 1914 the Russians lost 125,000 men; the Germans 15,000.

By the end of 1914, temporarily exhausted, the armies on the Western Front halted and dug in. It was the end of the dream of swift victory. The trenches soon stretched in an unbroken line from the Channel to the Swiss border. Over the next four years this line hardly shifted. As the war dragged on those who had half-welcomed it as an opportunity for glory and heroism became disillusioned. They saw the awful reality of modern war. Conditions in the trenches were appalling: soldiers fought, ate, and slept in mud among the corpses of their dead comrades, plagued by rats, lice, and artillery fire.

New weapons

Both sides sought to break the stalemate by introducing new weapons. In 1915 French soldiers, watching from the trenches, saw 'two curious greenish-yellow clouds on the ground which, moving before a light wind, became a bluish-white mist'. Terrified, the French soldiers began to run, coughing and pointing to their throats. The Germans had made the first use of poison gas on the battlefield. Gas was used widely by all sides during the war. Effective though it could be, it was difficult to control because of the wind. It was often impossible to produce a thick cloud of gas over a large enough area. There was also the danger that if the wind changed the gas could be blown back over friendly troops.

Warfare entered a new dimension with the use of air power. Aircraft were first used for reconnaissance; the invention of a device for synchronized firing between propellor blades led to battles between fighter aircraft.

The tank, introduced by the British in 1916, was another attempt to break the deadlock and return to mobile warfare. Its heavy caterpillar tracks could operate over even the roughest terrain, crushing barbed wire entanglements. Its crew, protected by the heavy steel armour on the outside of the tank, could destroy enemy machine-gunners. Used in large numbers the tank proved to be a devastating weapon.

Early in 1917 the USA entered the war

Above: Canadian troops repulse an attack at the second battle at Ypres, 1915. Massive frontal assaults proved disastrously wasteful during the First World War.

Right: By the end of the first year of the war, the Western Front had stabilized in a long line from the Belgian coast to the Swiss border. With very minor changes, this remained the shape of the front for the next four years.

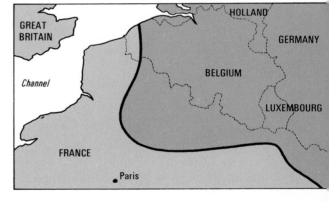

on the side of the Allies. This proved to be the turning point in the war. The battle-weary French and British troops 'Over There' on the Western Front were soon reinforced by a large, well-equipped American army; the Germans, on the other hand, had almost no reserves at all. Victory for the Allies was now certain.

On November 11, 1918, the war which was to have been over by Christmas four years earlier, finally came to an end.

The nations were exhausted: by the end of the war some 65 million men had been mobilized and 8 million had died. This did not include civilian losses. Three empires had fallen and the world had experienced warfare on a scale never before envisaged.

War in the Air

Aircraft have added a new dimension to warfare. Used first for reconnaissance, they soon took on a more active role as fighters and bombers. Today missile-carrying aircraft flying at twice the speed of sound patrol the skies.

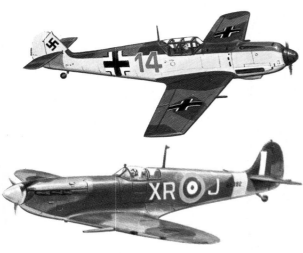

Top: The Spad – a favourite fighter aircraft of the First World War. Nearly 15,000 were built and flown by the French, Americans, Italians, and Belgians. With its 140 hp engine and twin Vickers machine guns, the Spad was a stable and fast machine and a deadly weapon in the hands of an experienced ace.

Above: The Fokker D-VII, built in 1918, was the best German fighter of the war. With a top speed of 120 mph and twin Spandau machine guns it was a match for the best of the Allies' aircraft.

Top: The German Messerschmitt Bf 109 outclassed all other fighters in the Second World War until the advent of the Spitfire. Its 1150 hp engine gave it a top speed of 357 mph and a ceiling of 36,000 feet.

Above: The British Supermarine Spitfire – one of the finest planes of the war. By the end of the war, a super Spitfire capable of 500 mph had been developed.

Right: The B-17 Flying Fortress was the main American bomber of the Second World War. These 30-ton machines were slow and relatively defenceless. One third of all the 13,000 built were shot down.
Far right: The V-2, unlike its predecessor the V-1, was a long-range rocket that travelled in a high arc trajectory against which there was no defence. But its bases were overrun in 1944 and it never became a serious threat.

During the late summer of 1914 a new sound was added to the cacophony of war on the Western Front: the drone of aircraft overhead. But aerial warfare was not entirely new. Long before the Wright Brothers had flown the first power-driven plane in 1903 successful military use had been made of balloons, kites, and small dirigibles.

First fighters

By the outbreak of the First World War in 1914 the British, French, Germans, Italians, and Americans all had air forces. But as the war leaders had not taken aircraft into account in planning their campaigns no one had a clear idea of how to use these new weapons. 'Aviation is a good sport,' declared the French commander General Foch, 'for the army it is useless.'

Aircraft were at first used to gather information by spotting enemy troop movements and artillery positions. Then gradually daring pilots in their fragile, slow planes began to take a more active part in the war. They dropped small bombs and grenades on enemy troops and attacked other aircraft – rather ineffectually with rifles, pistols, and shot guns! Then in 1915 the Germans invented an interrupter gear. This meant that a machine gun could be fitted to a plane which could fire between the propeller blades without hitting them.

This tremendous increase in fire power meant that many more planes were shot down. Men such as France's Georges Guynemer and Germany's Manfred von Richthofen became 'ace' pilots and popular heroes.

Quite early in the war long-range bombing raids were carried out by German Zeppelin airships and later by aircraft. The incendiary and high-explosive bombs caused more outrage than actual damage.

Defend, attack, support

After the First World War the two- and three-winged aircraft were largely replaced by sleek monoplane fighters and bombers capable of speeds of up to 360 mph. The remarkable power and awful effectiveness of these machines was first displayed in the Spanish Civil War, particularly in the German Luftwaffe's attack on the village of Guernica in northern Spain. The attack caused appallingly heavy losses of civilian lives. During the Second World War air power had three main roles. It had to drive the enemy's air force from the skies, bomb his towns and factories, and provide support for friendly forces on land and sea. In Germany's successful campaigns in Poland, Norway, Holland, and France in 1939 and 1940 fighter and bomber attacks caused panic among civilians and paralysed defending forces. In the attack on Britain in 1940 the Germans failed against the Royal Air Force's heavily outnumbered Spitfires and Hurricanes. Besides their courage and determination against overwhelming odds the British also had one great advantage – radar, which enabled German aircraft to be detected as they prepared to attack and gave the British time to intercept them.

Bombing raids caused enormous damage in the Second World War. But the systematic and devastating attacks on industrial and civilian targets by both sides seemed rather to strengthen than weaken morale. Towards the end of the war the Germans brought into play weapons they had been secretly developing. The deadly V2 rockets used to bombard London and the jet fighter aircraft might possibly, if they had been developed earlier, have forced the Allies to make peace. They failed; but they were terrible portents of the sort of weapons that could be expected in the future.

The Hawker Siddeley Harrier, the first fully operational vertical take-off fighter plane in the world. Its jet exhaust can be deflected downwards to give it vertical lift. Once airborne, its exhaust is adjusted for horizontal flight.

The Multi-Role Combat Aircraft (MRCA) is a European, swing-wing fighter bomber capable of a speed of more than twice the speed of sound.

War at Sea

The first ironclad ships appeared in the 19th century.
They were an answer to the new naval guns whose shells
could pierce wooden hulls with devastating ease.

The age of the wooden warship came to an end during the American Civil War. On March 8, 1862 the Confederate ironclad *Virginia* (formerly called *Merrimack*) steamed into battle at Hampton Roads. The cannonballs of the opposing Union (northern) fleet bounced harmlessly off her armoured hull. Returning next day the *Virginia* found a newly arrived Union ironclad, *Monitor*, waiting. The pitched gunfight that ensued was the first duel between ironclad men of war. But as neither ship's guns could penetrate the other's armour, the battle was inconclusive. The *Monitor* had one important advantage in this engagement – she carried the latest invention, a central revolving gun turret. After centuries, the age of broadside battle was over.

The armoured ship was the answer to the invention of a new naval gun that fired explosive shells that could pierce wooden

Above: Warships from the Second World War to the present. Modern warships have been greatly scaled down in size from the unwieldy monsters of 50 years ago. Small, fast cruisers and frigates and large nuclear submarines form the backbone of today's fleets.

Left: The first ironclad frigate was the French 'La Gloire'. Its wooden hull was armoured with 4½-inch plate. Though large for a frigate (5620 tons), its 900 hp engine could develop a speed of 13 knots, impressively fast for the time.

Below left: HMS 'Dreadnought' was the ultimate in battleship design when it appeared in 1906. It displaced nearly 18,000 tons, steamed at 21 knots, carried a battery of ten 12-inch guns, and was armoured with 11 inches of toughened steel plate.

hulls with devastating ease. In 1859 France launched *La Gloire*, an ironclad ship with a wooden hull. The first warship to be built entirely of iron was HMS *Warrior*. Despite her steam engine she carried a full set of sails. The first truly modern warship was HMS *Devastation*. Powered by a steam engine and driven by a screw propeller, her guns were housed in revolving turrets.

Another new weapon, the submarine, was first used in the American Civil War. These Davids, as they were called, carried an early type of torpedo. To deal with this new deadly weapon small, fast torpedo boats were built.

Outclassed
The navies of the world now sought a warship that was powerful enough to give them superiority over any other fleet.

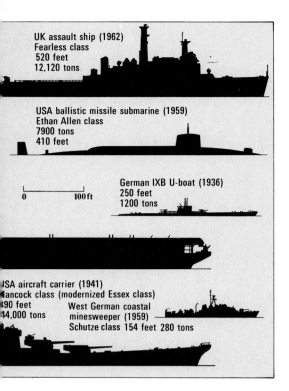

UK assault ship (1962)
Fearless class
520 feet
12,120 tons

USA ballistic missile submarine (1959)
Ethan Allen class
7900 tons
410 feet

0   100 ft

German IXB U-boat (1936)
250 feet
1200 tons

USA aircraft carrier (1941)
Hancock class (modernized Essex class)
890 feet
44,000 tons

West German coastal
minesweeper (1959)
Schutze class 154 feet 280 tons

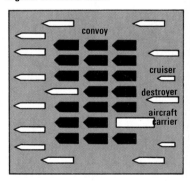

Modern guided missile destroyers are packed with sophisticated electronic gear and weaponry. A typical ship carries a range of surface-to-air and surface-to-surface missiles, anti-aircraft missiles, light calibre guns, anti-submarine weapons and a patrol helicopter.

The leaders in what was to become a 'naval race' were Germany and Great Britain. In 1906 Great Britain launched HMS *Dreadnought*, the first all-big-gun, heavily armoured, turbine-propelled battleship. It completely outclassed all other battleships. Germany immediately built ships of the dreadnought class. Yet only once, at the Battle of Jutland in 1916, did the dreadnoughts of Germany and Britain meet in a large-scale battle.

The greatest threat to a nation's supremacy at sea was the submarine. In both the First and Second World Wars German U-boat blockades and attacks on merchant ships brought Britain to the edge of defeat. The U-boat was finally beaten by the convoy system in which ships sailed in large numbers, escorted by fast warships and patrol aircraft.

Air power

Aircraft became important weapons in sea warfare in the Second World War. Operating either from shore bases or from aircraft carriers, they could hunt down and destroy both submarines and battleships. In May 1942 the Battle of Midway, one of the most decisive actions of the war, was fought between aircraft from Japanese and American carriers.

Today the submarine and aircraft carrier remain the most important weapons in sea warfare. The nuclear submarine can stay at sea for months and its missiles are capable of destroying targets thousands of miles inland. Destroyers, frigates, and fast patrol boats armed with surface-to-surface missiles protect the sea lanes. And so speed and mobility have replaced the towering might of the battleship.

The classic convoy of the Second World War consisted of an orderly rectangle of merchant vessels huddled under the watchful eye of an escort of swift destroyers, a small escort carrier, and frigates for rescue work.

convoy
cruiser
destroyer
aircraft carrier

Below: The French nuclear submarine 'Redoutable'.

Below: Aircraft carriers in the Mediterranean during the Second World War. The development of the aircraft carrier increased the striking range of a battle fleet to many hundreds of miles.

The Second World War

The Second World War was the first war to be fought on a world-wide scale – on land, on sea, and in the air.

In September 1939 Germany invaded Poland, and the Second World War began, ending hopes that the struggle of 1914 to 1918 had been the 'war to end all wars'.

This time the mood of the people was very different: soldiers left the barracks in grim silence; no bands played, no crowds cheered or threw flowers. What began as a land war in Europe soon became warfare on a world-wide scale; for the first time in history war was being fought simultaneously around the globe. Faster, more powerful aircraft and ships which could move troops quickly over great distances made this type of warfare possible.

'Blitzkrieg'

At the outset of the war the French and British commanders expected the land war to be similar to that of the First World War, with trenches and slow, massive attacks. They paid little attention to those who claimed that the improvements in weapons since 1918 made mobile warfare possible. The French insisted that 'the primary role of tanks will be the same as in the past, to assist the infantry in reaching their objectives'.

But the Germans saw that the old type of attack was too slow and costly. They made new fast tanks their chief weapon and adopted the *Blitzkrieg*, or 'lightning war', which aimed at defeating the enemy with as little fighting as possible. Instead of a general attack on the enemy defences the Germans punched a small hole in the defences with the aid of massed artillery and aircraft.

During the first three years of the war these tactics proved successful. Both the Germans and Russians, who saw the tank

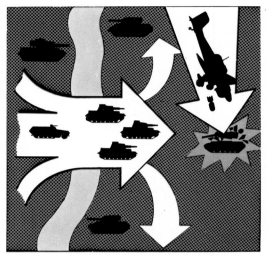

as the most efficient striking weapon, built large armoured forces. The British and Americans, on the other hand, felt that victory in battle would be achieved by combining all means of attack: tanks, artillery, mobile infantry, and air support. Tanks by themselves, they thought, would accomplish little. The difference in attitude was reflected in the types of tanks

Above: German Stukas enjoyed tremendous success in the early blitzkriegs in Poland, France, and Scandinavia.

Left: German blitzkrieg strategy was based on the mobility of strike forces. Dive bomber attacks prepared the way for the main thrust by spreading chaos behind the enemy lines. Then heavily armoured motorized forces were thrown against the weakest point in the defence to open a breach and pour through. Close behind the initial assault came infantry in trucks and armoured vehicles.

Below: Battles near Moscow, 1941. The deep snow and bitter cold of the Russian winter froze machinery and hampered troop movements. Soldiers wore special white camouflage against the snowy landscape. Below left: Allied troops take cover among the roots of a banyan tree during manoeuvres in Malaya. The armies fighting in the jungles of the Far East faced the constant threat of ambush from a hidden enemy.

built: German and Russian tanks were heavy with large guns and thick armour; the Americans and British built lighter, swift tanks.

Aircraft came into its own in the Second World War. Planes were adapted and equipped for long-range bombing, military transport, and reconnaissance. The striking power of the new air forces was demonstrated at Pearl Harbor in December 1941 when the surprise attack by Japanese carrier-launched planes and submarines crippled the US Pacific Fleet. The Germans developed the first effective long-range rockets used in warfare – the V2s.

Radar

An important breakthrough in warfare came with the invention of radar. Originally called Radio Detection and Ranging, radar was already being developed by the French, Germans, Americans, and British before the war. The threat of war accelerated research in Europe, particularly in Germany and Britain. Radar works by transmitting radio waves from a large aerial: if they meet a solid object, they bounce back like an echo and are picked up on a receiver. By measuring the time the wave takes to make its journey it is possible to work out how far away the object is. The direction, range, height, and speed of an oncoming aircraft or ship can all be calculated.

Although the Second World War produced far more sophisticated weapons than those used in any previous war, in some areas they could not be used. In arctic conditions the cold froze tank tracks and jammed the breeches of the guns. In the jungle war against Japan, soldiers had to develop special skills for survival and combat. Thick undergrowth, mountains, and swollen rivers often ruled out the use of heavy vehicles. Far more reliance was placed on the individual infantryman. In the desert, lack of water and swarms of flies made conditions unpleasant for men, while sand bogged down vehicles and found its way inside guns.

The Second World War was above all a battle of production. The side that could produce the most weapons was assured of victory: it was the Allies, with the great power of America and the Soviet Union, who finally overwhelmed Germany and Japan after six long years.

In the first week after D-Day, June 6, 1944, the Allies poured more than 325,000 men, 50,000 vehicles and 100,000 tons of equipment into northern Normandy. The attack punched a hole in Hitler's Atlantic Wall and brought the war to an end within a year.

Behind the Lines

The two great wars of this century have involved not just armies but entire nations. The mobilization of huge numbers of men and equipment demanded a united effort from all those left behind on the home front. 'A nation in arms' became the guiding principle.

Warfare in the 20th century has not been confined to battles at the front. Modern warfare involves civilian populations and what happens behind the lines can affect the entire course of the war. During the Second World War, both sides made much use of bombing raids to hit the enemy at home, as much to weaken his will as to destroy factories vital to the war effort. Many civilians were killed and injured: in Britain 60,000 people died in air attacks; in the German city of Dresden 100,000 lost their lives during bombing raids in February 1945; the Japanese cities of Hiroshima and Nagasaki were completely destroyed by the first atomic bombs used in warfare.

The war at home

At the beginning of the Second World War it was feared that poison gas might be used against civilian populations. Gas masks were issued to men, women, and children on the home front. Babies had special all-enclosing protection; masks were even available for dogs. Protection against high explosive and incendiary bombs was provided by specially built air-raid shelters, the cellars of strong buildings, and the tunnels of underground railways. In many cases children were evacuated from cities to areas where bombing was less likely; this often meant separation from their parents.

If people were to cope with the continual threat of air raids and with all the other strains of wartime, they had to have enough to eat. Governments recognized the importance of health and morale to the war effort. When attacks on shipping led to a huge drop in imports of basic foodstuffs, governments provided incentives to farmers to produce more food. They also rationed the amount of food that people could buy, so making sure that what was available was distributed fairly.

The ability of women to do men's work had been proven in the First World War, when European and American women

Above left: In a last ditch attempt to save the city, Russian women were given military drilling as German forces approached Moscow. Training the civilian population to fight as the last line of resistance gave a new meaning to the idea of 'a nation in arms'.

Left: Japanese women work in a munitions factory during the Second World War. The desperate shortage of men made it necessary for women to go to work, even in societies like Japan where traditionally it was unheard of.

went to work in munitions factories. But their contribution during the Second World War was on a much larger scale, and in traditional societies like Japan the switch to a war economy revolutionized the position of women. Women acted as air-raid wardens, ambulance drivers, and fire-fighters. They kept transport and postal services running and worked in factories turning out ships, tanks, aircraft, chemicals, and munitions. Others joined reserve units attached to the armed forces.

Most countries organized home defence units – a part-time army made up of those too old, too young, or unfit to join the

Right: Russian peasants flee before the German advance on Moscow. Refugees made homeless by war are the innocent victims of armed conflict.

Left: In Britain the threat of invasion led to the organization of a Home Guard. Here, they drill with broom handles. Such home defence units were organized by a number of countries in the Second World War.

Below left: An all-enclosing protection against gas for babies. At the beginning of the Second World War it was feared that gas would be used against civilians.

Below: A jungle POW camp for Japanese prisoners. Though the treatment of prisoners of war varied considerably during the Second World War, it was to some degree controlled by international agreement.

regular army, and those in 'reserved occupations' – jobs vital to the war effort. In occupied countries unofficial underground movements adopted guerrilla tactics to harrass and sabotage the enemy at every opportunity, even if it meant destroying their own factories.

Captured resistance workers, if they escaped shooting, were often sent to one of a number of civilian concentration camps. Conditions in the German camps were appalling: millions of prisoners were executed or died of starvation. Captured soldiers, sailors, and airmen on both sides were usually better treated. They were held in special prisoner-of-war (POW) camps, where conditions were tolerable and were to some degree monitored by the International Red Cross.

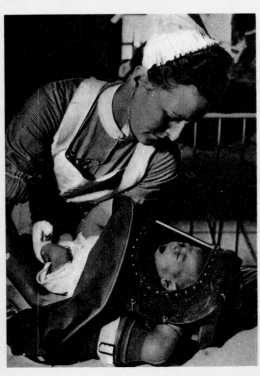

The Balance of Power

The Cold War and the nuclear stalemate have changed the nature of warfare. In some parts of the world the conventional soldier has been replaced by the guerrilla.

Above: A United Nations peace-keeping force stationed on the west bank of the Suez Canal separates two opposing armies in an attempt to reduce the chances of a clash. Although the UN force itself is too weak to affect the outcome of any full-scale battle, its presence on the scene is a constant reminder that the rest of the world is determined to avoid the outbreak of another major war.

Right: A NATO radar station in northern Turkey, part of a defensive network that runs from the Arctic to the Mediterranean.

In the years following the Second World War the USA and the Soviet Union emerged as the two most powerful nations in the world – the 'superpowers'. Although these two nations had been allies during the Second World War, their opposed political ideas and different foreign policy aims soon brought them into conflict. To present a united front the USA and the countries of Western Europe formed the North Atlantic Treaty Organization (NATO) in 1949; in 1955 the Soviet Union and the Communist countries of Eastern Europe formed the Warsaw Pact. The differences between East and West have not so far resulted in a Third World War, but in a series of world crises which have come to be known as the Cold War.

The Cold War

The first crisis of the Cold War occurred in occupied Berlin, Germany, in 1948 when the Soviets blockaded the city. Two years later United Nations forces, more than 90 per cent of whom were American, went to the defence of South Korea which had been invaded by the Communist North. In 1956 the Soviet Union's invasion of Hungary and the Anglo-French invasion of Egypt over the Suez Canal caused tension within the alliances as well as between them. But in 1962 the most serious crisis flared up when the Soviet Union attempted to install nuclear missiles on Cuba, within range of the USA. For several tense days the world was on the brink of nuclear war. An American later said that they had 'looked into the mouth of the cannon'. But both sides realized the devastation a nuclear war would bring, and so the balance of terror remained.

The possibility of nuclear war is still with us. The balance of power is less stable as the number of countries with nuclear weapons has increased, despite some successful attempts at arms control. A Nuclear Test Ban Treaty was signed in 1963; the USA and the Soviet Union continue to hold Strategic Arms Limitation Talks (SALT).

The United Nations was established after the Second World War as an international forum for settling disputes with the power to enforce its rulings militarily if necessary. But the UN has failed to win

the complete support it requires to function properly. It has acted most effectively as a neutral policing agency, separating warring factions in various trouble-spots.

Guerrilla warfare

Real power remains in the hands of the two great superpowers, who continue to support their allies in the 'Third World' of developing nations. In the 1960s the USA became involved in a costly war in South-east Asia when it attempted to stop Communist North Vietnam from taking over the South. In the Middle East the USA has played the role of peacemaker between Israel and the Arab states.

Faced with the nuclear stalemate, the nature of warfare, especially in the developing countries, has changed. Nationalist movements in many countries have made increasing use of guerrilla warfare, often the only effective means of undermining a strong military power. Guerrillas aim to force changes in a political system through terror and destruction directed at 'soft' civilian targets as well as military installations and personnel. Operating in a city they are known as 'urban guerrillas'; their most important weapons include the bomb and the booby trap.

Regular armies, with all the fire power and manpower at their command, have been unable to combat guerrilla tactics effectively. Conventional weapons and warfare are of little use against the lightning strikes of a hidden enemy.

Far left: American troops await an attack in Korea. United Nations-US intervention in Korea in 1950 made that country one of the first hotspots in the Cold War.

Left: Frelimo guerrillas in Mozambique. Guerrilla warfare has become a feature of nationalist movements since the Second World War.

Below: The annual Mayday parade in Moscow's Red Square is an impressive military review held to commemorate the Russian Revolution. Soldiers, tanks, and rockets sweep past the Soviet leaders in the review stand. New Soviet weapons are often unveiled on this occasion.

Glossary of Terms

**Decoration Militaire
(Belgium)**

**Purple Heart
(USA)**

**Iron Cross
(Germany)**

**Order of Victory
(USSR)**

A

Armada A Spanish word meaning a fleet of warships.

Artillery General name for all cannon, guns, and howitzers. It is also that branch of an army specializing in such weapons.

B

Ballista A large catapult, shaped like a crossbow, for shooting heavy missiles. It was invented by the Romans.

Bayonet A metal stabbing weapon, spiked or knife shaped, fixed to the muzzle of a rifle or musket. It was first used in the 17th century as a 'plug' bayonet, fitting into the muzzle; later it was fixed round the outside of the muzzle so it did not have to be removed for firing.

Bireme A galley used in ancient times, especially by the Romans, with two banks of oars.

Blitzkrieg German for 'lightning war'; refers to the swift attack used by German forces early in the Second World War.

Bore The inside of the barrel of a firearm.

Breech The rear end of a gun barrel. A weapon loaded through the breech is called a 'breech-loader'.

Broadside The simultaneous firing of all guns on one side of a warship.

Bushido The code of moral principles followed by Japanese samurai.

C

Camouflage The disguising of men, installations, and fighting vehicles so that they blend in with their surroundings and cannot be spotted easily.

Cartridge A cylindrical container of paper or metal containing a ball or bullet and a charge of powder. Modern cartridges also include a percussion cap.

Cavalry Horse soldiers, or the mounted regiments of an army.

Chivalry The code of conduct by which warriors lived and fought during the Middle Ages.

Column A battle formation of troops usually narrower than its length. Napoleon's columns, however, were usually solid squares, 30 men deep.

Corps A major military unit: an army of 50,000 might be divided into two corps, each containing three or four divisions.

Crossbow a bow placed across a wooden stock and wound back mechanically to fire short iron bolts.

D

Division A large unit of an army, containing infantry, cavalry, artillery, and all supporting services.

Drawbridge A bridge that can be raised to prevent its being used by an enemy, usually for crossing a moat.

E

Enlistment The act of joining one of the armed services.

F

Flank The side of an army or fleet drawn up in line of battle.

Flint A hard stone used to strike a spark in early firearms — hence *flintlock*.

Front Where the fighting is. The front lines are those tactical positions nearest the enemy's.

G

Galleass A large, fast, three-masted warship with at least 30 cannon, introduced by the Venetians and used in the 16th and 17th centuries.

Galleon A heavy square-rigged sailing ship with high stem and stern, used especially by the Spanish from the 15th to 17th centuries.

Galley A long, narrow, single-decked vessel of the Mediterranean propelled by oars ranged in banks on either side.

Guerrilla Spanish for 'little war'; member of an irregular military force which operates in small groups, using the tactics of terror, sabotage, propaganda, and raids.

H

Halberd An axe and spike mounted on a long shaft, used during the 15th and 16th centuries.

Hoplite A heavy infantryman of Ancient Greece.

I

Incendiary bomb A bomb containing chemicals that ignite on contact to spread fire.

Infantry Soldiers trained and equipped to fight on foot.

J

Joust A contest between armoured knights with lances on horseback, often as part of a tournament.

K

Keep The inner tower and main stronghold of a medieval castle.

L

Lance A spear carried by horsemen; regiments equipped with these were known as lancers.

Legion Roman infantry force of up to 6000, supported by cavalry and engines of war.

Line formation An arrangement of soldiers with a broad front and narrow depth, so allowing more soldiers to fire simultaneously.

Lock The firing mechanism of a musket.

Longbow Powerful medieval bow about six feet long, normally of yew.

M

Mace A club with a spiked or ridged head and a metal or wooden handle.

Mercenary A professional soldier who fights for money, regardless of the nationality of his employer.

Middle Ages The period between the 5th and 15th centuries AD.

Militia Part-time soldiers whose duty is home defence.

Moat A ditch, often full of water, surrounding a castle or other fortified place.

Mobilization The process of getting an army ready for active service on the outbreak of a war.

Munitions Armaments or ammunition in the manufacturing or storing stage.

Musket A smooth-barrelled shoulder firearm.

Muzzle The mouth of the barrel of a firearm, from which the bullet emerges.

N

Nuclear weapon One whose explosive force comes from the fusion or fission of atomic nucleii.

P

Parallel A trench intended to give a covered approach to a fortress or town that is under siege.

Partisan Member of a guerrilla band which makes forays and generally harrasses an invading enemy force.

Percussion cap A small explosive charge or detonator fired by a sharp blow that sets off the main charge of a firearm.

Phalanx A solid square formation of infantry used by the early Greeks and perfected by the Macedonians under Philip and Alexander the Great.

Pike A weapon up to 18 feet long consisting of a long wooden shaft tipped with a pointed metal head. Used by infantry until the end of the 18th century.

Ports Openings with hinged covers in the sides of ships, hence 'gun-ports' for the cannon.

Prime To prepare a musket for firing by putting a small amount of gunpowder in the priming pan which will be used to set off the charge.

R

Radar 'Radio Detection and Ranging'; a device for locating an object by means of ultra high frequency radio waves. It is used in warfare for tracking the direction, range, height, and speed of such things as ships and aircraft.

Recoil The sharp backward movement of a firearm caused by the explosion of the charge.

Reconnaissance A military survey of territory.

Rifling Spiral grooves cut into the barrel of a firearm to make the bullet spin so it travels more accurately to the target.

S

Sabotage Damage caused to installations, factories, railways, usually by resistance groups or those politically opposed to the central authority.

Siege A military attack and blockade of a town or fortification intended to force its surrender.

Skirmisher A foot soldier trained to fight independently in front of the main force, so disrupting the enemy's preparations and making him more vulnerable to attack.

Square formation Arrangement of infantry into a hollow square for receiving a cavalry charge.

Strategy The planning of movements of armies to achieve overall war aims.

T

Tactics The art of manoeuvring troops on the battlefield, or in the presence of the enemy.

Tournament A medieval gathering for knightly sports, jousts and tilts, often lasting several days.

Service Medal with
'Korea' clasp (United Nations)

Victoria Cross
(Great Britain)

Medal of Honor
(USA)

Croix de Guerre
(France)

Index

Acknowledgments
Photographs: Page 2 United Nations/Y. Nagata (top), Michael Holford/Victoria and Albert Museum (centre), Bulloz/Musée de l'Armée, Paris (bottom); 3 Wallace Collection (top right), Picturepoint (bottom); 4 British Museum (top left), Michael Holford/British Museum (centre & bottom left), Sonia Halliday (bottom right); 5 Wallace Collection (top), Imperial War Museum (centre left), Associated Press (centre right), Ministry of Defence (bottom); 6 Peter Clayton (top & centre right), British Museum (bottom); 7 British Museum (top); 8 Michael Holford/British Museum; 9 Michael Holford/British Museum; 11 Statens Historiska Museum, Stockholm; 13 Michael Holford/British Museum; 14 William MacQuitty (top), Michael Holford/Victoria and Albert Museum (bottom left), Japan Information Centre (bottom right); 15 Victoria and Albert Museum (top); 16 Victoria and Albert Museum (top), Bodleian Library (bottom); 19 J. Allan Cash (top), Sonia Halliday (centre), Crown Copyright, Department of the Environment (bottom); 20 RTHPL; 21 RTHPL; 22 National Maritime Museum, London (top), Mary Evans Picture Library (bottom); 24 National Army Museum, London (top), Musées de la Ville de Strasbourg (bottom); 25 National Army Museum, London (top right); 26 National Army Museum, London; 27 Mary Evans Picture Library (top), International Red Cross, Geneva (centre); 28 Mansell Collection (top & bottom), John Freeman/British Museum (background); 29 Popperfoto (left), Mansell Collection (right); 30 National Portrait Gallery, London (centre), National Army Museum, London (bottom left & right); 31 Bulloz/Musée de l'Armée, Paris (top), Science Museum, London (bottom); 32 RTHPL; 33 RTHPL, London; 34 RTHPL, London; 35 National Army Museum, London; 36 Imperial War Museum; 37 Hawker Siddeley; 38 Mansell Collection (top), Imperial War Museum (bottom); 39 U.S. Navy (top), Imperial War Museum (bottom left), E.C.P.-Armées (right); 40 Imperial War Museum (top), Novosti Press Agency (bottom left), Imperial War Museum (bottom right); 42 Novosti Press Agency (top), Imperial War Museum (bottom); 43 Novosti Press Agency (top right), Imperial War Museum (top left), Popperfoto (bottom right), Imperial War Museum (bottom left); 44 United Nations/Y. Nagata (top), NATO (bottom); 45 Popperfoto (top), Camera Press (centre), Novosti Press Agency (bottom).
Artwork: Faulkner/Marks Partnership. Diagrams on page 29 based on diagrams appearing in *The Art of Warfare on Land* by David Chandler (The Hamlyn Publishing Group Ltd.). Cover: Richard Hook
Picture Research: Penny Warn and Jackie Newton